SAMPSON LOW

ng
arden

a visual guide
by the DIAGRAM GROUP
featuring specially
designed gardens by
ROBIN WILLIAMS

Foreword

The English landscape garden designer Robin Williams was commissioned to plan a number of gardens that feature some particular aspect of garden design, and offer solutions to a number of specific problems of site or function. Most gardens contain a variety of problems, and most families want to use their garden for a number of purposes. We hope that the reader will be able to pick out the ideas that will solve his own particular problems from among the numerous ideas in this book.

Each of Robin Williams' gardens is presented in an initial large drawing, with certain of its features explained or elaborated in the text or on a later page. Try to think yourself into the gardens: they have all been drawn as if viewed from above and to one side (from the attic

First published in 1978 by
Sampson Low, Berkshire House,
Queen Street, Maidenhead,
Berkshire SL6 1NF

© Diagram Visual Information Ltd
All rights reserved
Printed by Purnell & Sons Ltd

SBN 562 00102 6

window of the house next door, perhaps), so that you can see most of the elements at the same time; but if you were standing in the garden at ground level you would get a completely different view, and a more partial one. One of the great pleasures of walking around a garden is the discovery of corners that were hidden from your sight at first. And one of the joys of planning a garden is to design such pleasant surprises for one's visitors. But don't try to cram too many ideas into one small garden; and don't be too ambitious. A modest success is better than a spectacular failure.

And finally, remember Kipling's well-known lines, that 'gardens are not made, By singing Oh how beautiful! and sitting in the shade.'

A distinctive feature of Planning Your Garden *is that throughout the book a wise old owl makes occasional helpful suggestions to improve your garden or to lighten your work.*

The Diagram Group

Editors	Maureen Cartwright, Elizabeth Wilhide
Art Editor	Richard Hummerstone
Artists	Stephen Clark, Robert Galvin, Brian Hewson, Susan Kinsey, Pavel Kostal, Janos Marffy, Kathleen McDougall, Graham Rosewarne
Consultants	G. W. Ace, Barbara Haynes
Picture Credits	The Mansell Collection Le Corbusier/Ullstein Mirror Group Newspapers

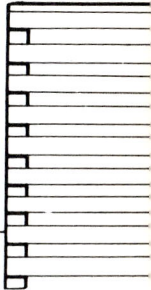

Contents

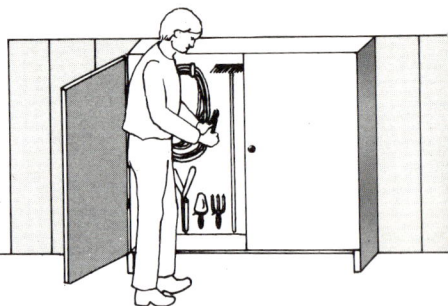

Chapter one
Garden planning

Since early times man has grown crops around his home, but it was much later when he began to grow flowers purely for pleasure, and to worry about the layout of the whole garden. Many poor folk had a small plot of land, but it is only the large gardens of monasteries and castles that we know about now from old books.

The Benedictine monastery of St Gall in Switzerland had extensive gardens as early as the 9th century: a cloister garth with lawns and paths, where the monks took some exercise; a physic garden of herbs; a vegetable garden; and an orchard. Although they paid attention to the layout of the gardens, they were concerned with the practical requirements of medicine and food, not with any aesthetic considerations. Most monasteries also had ponds where the monks caught the fish that supplied their meals on fast-days. Many large houses had moats around them, primarily for fortification, but these were also a source of fish for the table.

The 13th-century *Roman de la Rose*, both through its text and by the many illustrations in various manuscripts, gives a clear idea of the ideal version of the castle gardens then popular. The garden was enclosed with walls and a moat, and divided by trellises. The lawns, dotted with flowers, were shaded by fruit trees, and there was a fountain made of copper in the middle, set in a circular pool; the water from this pool ran away along a narrow marble channel across the lawn, and into the moat outside. The beds were edged with stone coping, and contained clipped shrubs and flowers. The flower beds were often raised several inches above the path, and these paths were covered with sand. Sometimes a wooden bower or arbour was covered with climbing plants to provide a shady seat. The wall around the garden was at first made of stone, but later brick was introduced for this purpose, and hedges also came into use. There was also a massive locked gate to some gardens, when they were within a castle. Inside the garden, the trellis fences were often covered with roses, though not the hybrids we know today.

Contemporary gardens
depicted in mediaeval
manuscripts.

When the long Wars of the Roses eventually came to an end, many castles fell into disuse, and people began to plan their new homes with convenience and enjoyment in mind, rather than the demands of fortification. They built on slopes or in valleys, rather than on the windy inaccessible hilltops that had been the ideal site for a mediaeval castle (and the worst possible site for a garden, necessitating the high walls to protect plants from the wind).

The gardens at Hampton Court were completely remodelled by Henry VIII. One of the many innovations was a mount, built on a foundation of brick, covered with earth. This was so large that it had a summerhouse on its summit, from which visitors could see over the wall to the outside world. Many devices such as sun dials and carved animals of wood or stone were placed around the gardens, and there were also special areas for playing at bowls and for practising archery. But flower gardens were not common until the reign of Elizabeth I. Knot gardens were planted with fairly low-growing plants, outlined with neat hedges made of box, yew or lavender, and arranged in elaborate designs. Topiary work was very popular, and sometimes fantastic shapes were created, but many hedges were cut straight, and these formed an excellent foil for the bright flowers. The really large gardens must have needed an army of servants to keep them in order.

The discovery of many foreign lands, and especially of the New World, led to many quite new plants being brought home by travellers and tried out in their gardens in England; many of these flourished, and have been with us ever since. Gerard's famous *Herball* was published in 1597, and many similar works were written in an attempt to catalogue the increasing number of plants available to the gardener. Besides lists of old and new plants, these Herbals also included advice on how the plants should be grown. A French writer of 1603 suggested having four divisions in the garden: the kitchen garden, one for cut flowers, one for herbs, and an orchard.

The two Tradescants, father and son, were importing many new plants from the New World at this period. In 1632 the first botanical garden was founded at Oxford University; by 1648 it contained 1600 different kinds of plants.

Gardens continued to evolve slowly, and some changes were due to various influences from France, Italy and the Netherlands. Statues and vases made of lead were adopted from the French fashion, and so were wrought-iron gates. Around this time, flowers became less popular, and many gardens consisted of little but lawns, gravel paths and shrubs. When flowers were grown, they were often rare specimens, and were planted in pots or urns, not in the ground. The French designer Le Nôtre started making vast estates with innumerable statues and fountains, and large sheets of water, and this fashion spread to England. Grottoes were a temporary craze, many lined with shells or fragments of glass. Mock ruins and classical temples were built on many English estates.

De Vries 1532 garden design: note the lattice-work fences.

In the 18th century the landscape garden became popular. Kent was the first to react against the fashion for formality, and he was soon followed by 'Capability' Brown and Humphry Repton. Repton wrote a very famous book about landscape gardening, published in 1803, and this had an enormous influence on garden fashions. Repton himself, unlike many of his followers, had great respect for the past, and tried to match the garden to the building, instead of following fashion blindly and destroying the traditional gardens of the past.

Around this time there was a great deal of interest in China. A number of books were written about oriental gardening, and these had some influence. The Chinese venerated the natural landscape, and tried to create seemingly natural features in their gardens. The Chinese fashion eventually led to the building of pagodas and the construction of the Royal Pavilion at Brighton, but on the whole it reinforced the movement towards naturalism.

During all these changes, the cottager was comparatively unaffected. He grew as much as he could cram into his small piece of land, and it was always useful crops that he grew, to help to make life easier for himself and his large family. The poor man grew useful vegetables and herbs, and if there *were* any flowers, they were usually crowded into odd corners.

With the industrial revolution, the middle classes in the suburbs became interested in gardening, and many quite small houses had a conservatory at the side, where exotic plants were grown for the house, including the notorious aspidistra. House-owners aped the big houses of an earlier age with terraces, balustrades and urns on a smaller scale, but they had a genuine interest in growing flowers of all kinds.

With the crowding of the cities and the arrival of the motorcar, a reversal soon began, and wealthy people often moved out to the country, where they bought old cottages and grew old-fashioned flowers in the garden, although many of them also kept a vegetable patch.

Nowadays, we can see gardens in all shapes and sizes and styles. Many of the big country houses open their gardens to the public, and some owners of modest cottage gardens also allow visitors once or twice a year for a Good Cause. Such gardens are often beyond the scope of the average amateur, because they usually need plenty of money or plenty of labour (or both) to bring them to such perfection. But the visitor can often gain a few tips on how to improve his own more modest garden. From the most elaborate flower bed, you can get ideas about which kinds of flowers would look good together in a window-box.

The modern gardener also has many advantages that were denied the builders of the great estates of the past. A vast assortment of tools is available, for instance, including lawn mowers and hedge clippers. Chemicals of many kinds help to keep the soil healthy, and selective weedkillers save a good deal of work. Professional gardeners are hard to come by, and expensive, but most small gardens can be kept neat and pleasant by the family, without outside help.

Many new varieties of flowers and vegetables have been developed by horticulturists, and this means a better show or an increased yield for gardeners without extra effort. Compare the tiny wild daffodil with the cultivated ones, or a wild strawberry with the latest varieties. Some new varieties are more resistant to disease than their ancestors; and even if they succumb, there are usually chemicals available to combat the infection.

This book attempts to show you some of the many possibilities available when you plan your garden. Many of the designs may well look far too large to be within your reach, if you have only a tiny plot; but the basic problems are very similar, and you will still have to test your soil, and grow the same plants, and make paths or a fence. If you have only a tiny area, there is an even better chance of keeping it all in perfect order, and many an owner of acres would envy you the problems.

Making a plan

Faced with a strange garden that has suddenly become your responsibility, you may well feel daunted. Your first decision will be whether to do all the work alone or to call in an expert to help. This may depend partly on the state of the land you have acquired: if it has been lovingly cared for by an enthusiast, you can go along with the existing garden, at least for the first year or two, discovering which ideas are right for you and which need to be changed. If you are faced instead with a new plot buried in rubble and junk, you may be rather daunted, but it won't just go away, so you had better start on it as soon as possible.

Whether you intend to lay out your new garden yourself or to get professional help, the first step is the same: test the soil (page 20), because this is the basis on which much will depend. Then you can draw a detailed plan of the existing features, showing the garden's size and limits (see below), and drawing in your ideas. Or you can turn to a professional for help.

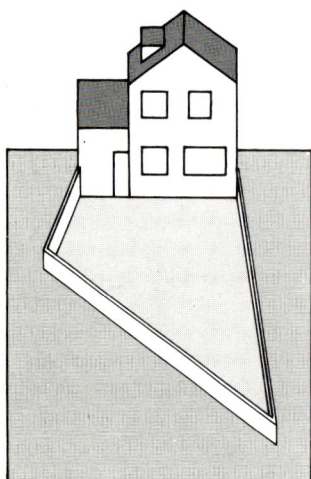

If your house is fairly new, you may be able to get a plan of the plot from the architect who designed it or from the public authority that approved it. If not, you can make your own plan. Start measuring from a fixed line: usually the back wall of the house is easiest. Draw the back wall line to a chosen scale, perhaps ¼ in to 1 ft. So if the wall

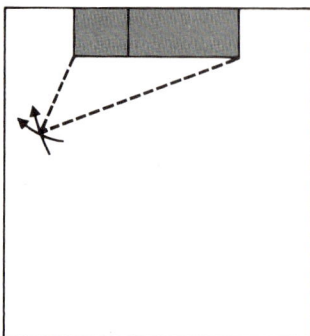

measures 30 ft, draw a line 7½ in long. Then measure the distances from the house to the boundaries; if the plot is square and the boundaries are parallel to the house wall, you will find this simple. If not, you must use the method above, called triangulation. Measure the distance of a corner of the boundary from each corner of the

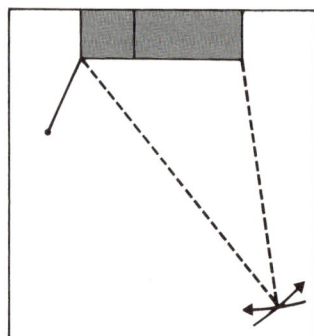

house wall. Suppose the point is 16 ft from one corner of the house and 40 ft from the other. Using compasses, make an arc 4 in (16 ft) from one corner, then an arc 10 in (40 ft) from the other end of the house wall. Where they cross is the boundary mark. Plot all the corners of the boundaries in this way.

If you decide to call in a landscape architect to help to plan your garden, one of the first things to discuss is money. This ensures that you do not receive a bill which you cannot afford. Initially, you will have to pay for him to travel between his office and your garden, and a consultancy fee. For this, he will look at your garden, discuss with you what you have already decided, and try to merge your needs and his own expert knowledge into a working plan. After you have paid the landscape architect, the plan he has drawn up becomes your property. The plan will show all the existing tangible features of the garden (boundaries, trees, paths if any) and also the additional features that you and the landscape architect have worked out.

If your garden is small, this does not necessarily mean that the plan will be much cheaper than if it was large. In fact, it is often much harder to plan a small area, because it is hard to hide things away, and because every square foot must be used.

When you are planning a garden (with or without professional help), you must bear in mind a number of restricting factors. It is no good drawing up elaborate plans and then finding that they are impossible because of local byelaws or because neighbours object. So try to consider all the snags before you begin to plan.

Factors to remember when planning your garden

Planning permission This may be needed for any permanent structure over 6 ft (1.8 m) in height. Consult the local planning authority (ask at your Town Hall) before starting work. The local byelaws vary from one area to another; make careful enquiries about these before you make plans.

Right of way If a footpath crosses your land, there may be a permanent right of way, and you will not be able to prevent people from using it.

Neighbours Your neighbours deserve some consideration, if you expect them to consider you too. Do not plant trees that will overhang their property or darken their house. Site your barbecue where smoke will not annoy them.

Smokeless zones If you live in a smokeless zone you cannot have a bonfire.

Costs The expense of your new garden will no doubt be a matter of concern to you. Bear in mind not only the initial outlay, but also the cost of maintenance, which can often amount to more in the end.

Courses of action

Now that you have your plan, there are four possible courses of action you can take:

1 You can do all the work yourself from the plan, if you have the necessary skills.

2 You can do part of the work yourself, but call in a contractor to do certain difficult jobs.

3 You can hand the plan to a contractor and he will do all the work under your supervision.

4 You can hand the whole job to a contractor, to be done under the supervision of the landscape architect who drew up the plan.

Hard landscaping is the structural part of making a garden: walls, patio, pool, etc. Soft landscaping is the selecting and planting of flowers, grass and trees. Many people call in expert help for the hard landscaping, but do the soft landscaping themselves.

If you decide to employ a landscape contractor you must ask him for an estimate of the cost of implementing the plan. A good contractor can work from a sufficiently detailed plan, without costly additional specifications.

If you employ a contractor, you may decide to choose one who is a member of a bona fide association of landscape contractors. There are many other contractors, however, some of whom have little experience: in fact, they could well be learning their trade on your garden, and may not be wholly competent. They may be slightly cheaper than a recognized contractor, if you decide to take the risk; but they could well prove to be more costly, if anything goes wrong.

If you employ a good contractor, you can leave the whole job to him, or try to supervise it yourself (which is difficult if you are at work all the week), or employ the landscape architect to supervise the contractor: for this job, he will charge about 10% of the total contractor's bill, for approving the quality of the work, checking the contractor's accounts on your behalf, and checking progress.

Some landscape architects have connections with a firm of contractors who will carry out their plans if you wish.

" Every man to 'is fancy—I grow weeds "

Starting from scratch

If you have moved into a new house, your 'garden' is likely to be covered in builders' rubble. If you are lucky, there may be a few trees, but these could be in the wrong place. You may have taken over a garden that has been left for many years or that does not suit your requirements or appeal to your imagination. There is even a possibility that you would like to improve or change a garden you have worked on for some time. All these situations are good opportunities to 'start from

All the features shown below could present problems of planning, upkeep or design. Each is dealt with in a different section of the book: for easy reference the relevant pages are given here to help in locating the right solution.

scratch' and take note of different possibilities. Discuss the matter carefully with all of the members of your family: each of them will be using the garden, and each will have views on how it should be. A word with the neighbours may help too, especially if they have lived there longer than you have: they may know, for instance, that your predecessor tried to do the same thing that you are planning, but it didn't work out. But when you have consulted everyone make up your own mind!

14 Play area, pages 114–7
15 Drainage, pages 24–5
16 Slope, pages 28–9
17 Eyesores, page 133
18 Vegetable patch, pages 138–9
19 Compost heap, page 119

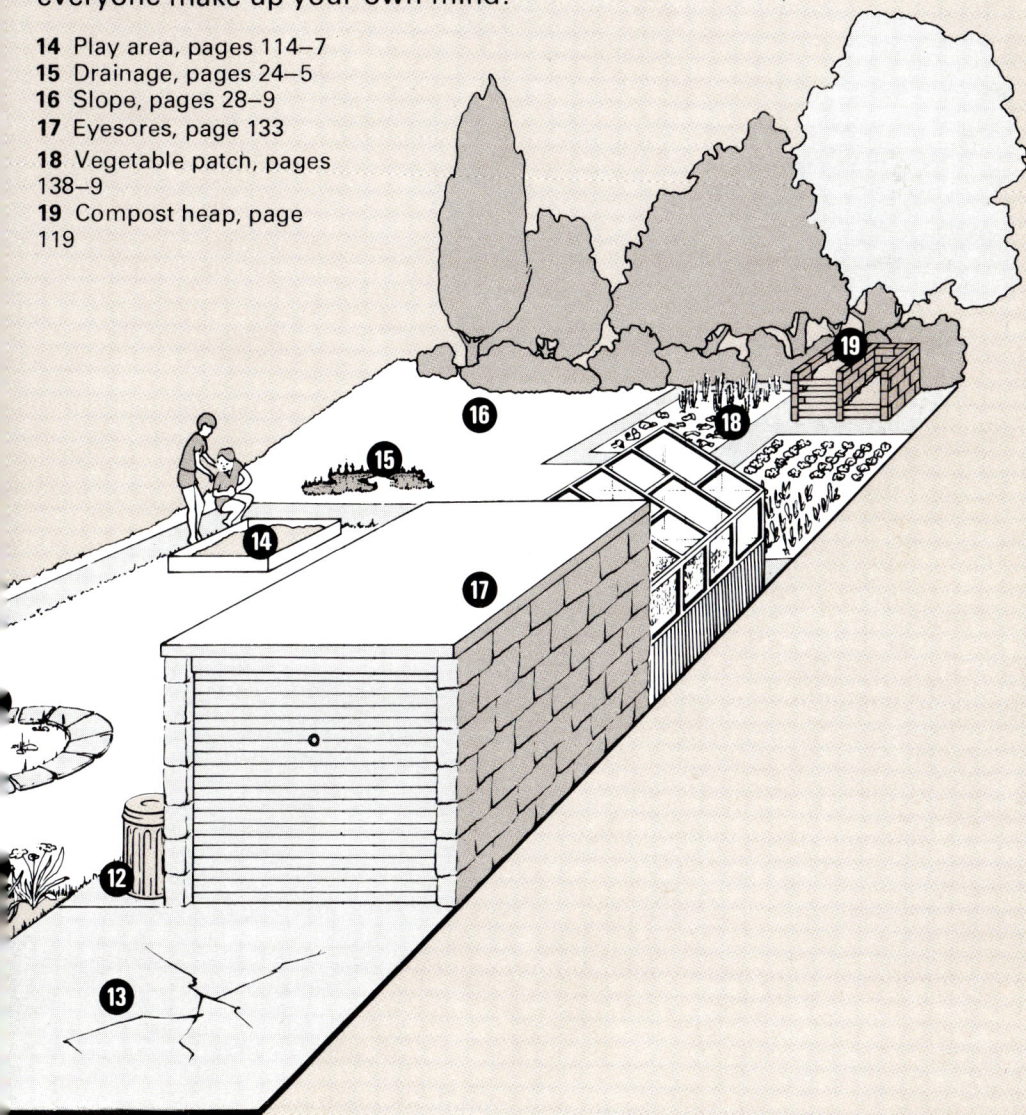

Choosing the elements

Many people like drawing plans and making lists better than actually getting down to the digging, and it is certainly true that too much planning is not necessarily a good thing, but during the long winter evenings no one can be accused of laziness, and it is well to be ready to start work as soon as the weather allows, with all one's seeds and equipment ready. And if you send away for seeds, there may be a delay in receiving them by post. Make sure you have everything you need, so that when the sun shines you can start digging.

It is often necessary to work out the area of a piece of land, for calculating how much seed you need to make a lawn, for instance. The job is easy if the piece of land is square or oblong: just measure the length and the breadth, and multiply them together. So a lawn 6 yards long and 5 yards broad covers 30 square yards. (See page 140 for help in conversions.) Most people now have quite small gardens, and the soil is similar all over; but if you have a big garden you should test the soil in several places, as the land may vary widely.

You can buy a soil-testing kit to test the alkalinity or acidity of the soil. Strips of treated paper are dipped into a mixture of soil and water, and their colour is then measured against a pH scale, which goes from 0 to 14. If soil is above 7 on the scale, it is alkaline; under 7 the soil is acid. To restore the soil balance, acid soil needs 8–12 oz (0.2–0.3 kg) of lime to each square yard or square metre of land. Alkaline soil needs compost and peat, and some sulphate of ammonia or flowers of sulphur.

Soil kits also tell you which plant foods are present. Plants need nitrogen, phosphorus and potassium, and traces of other elements. If soil lacks these, plants will not thrive (pages 26–7). You will need to calculate the area of beds to work out how much lime or fertilizer you need to buy. For instance, you should allow about 4 oz (112 g) of bone meal to each square yard or square metre, whereas sulphate of potash is needed in smaller amounts: about 1 oz (28 g) to each square yard or square metre.

This book contains lots of garden ideas, and no garden could possibly include them all. Look through, and see which suits your land, your tastes and your purse. If you are new to gardening, don't be too ambitious: it is better to make a success of a simple scheme than an elaborate disaster. And hard work *does* work wonders.

The nature of the site is very important in dictating your finished garden. You must examine the soil, and bear in mind the slope of the land (see pages 28–9) and its aspect. The shape and size of the garden also partly dictate what you can plan to include, and your scheme must take all these factors into consideration.

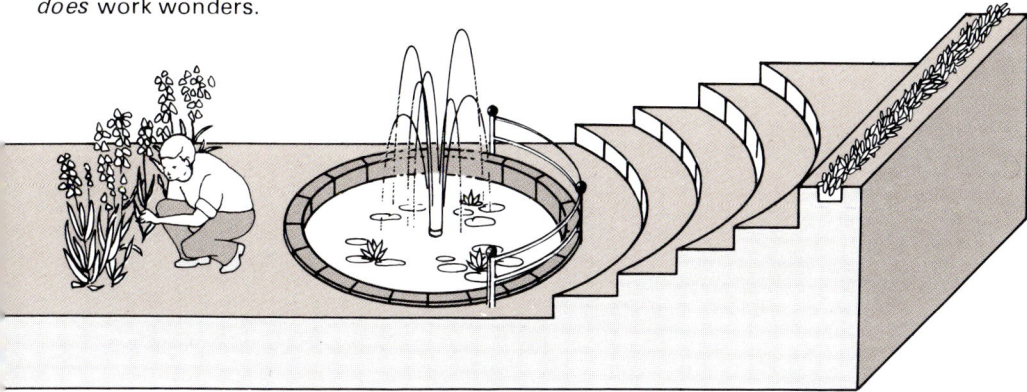

When planning what to grow where, you must take the needs of all into account: it is unfair to plant vegetables where your son has played cricket for the last 2 summers and expect them to be left in peace! The plants have needs too, so choose a sunny spot for those that enjoy sunshine, and provide shade for those that need it. And when planning your garden, always bear in mind the size that plants, shrubs and trees will reach when they mature: trees are easier to plant than to get rid of, 30 years later (see pages 86–7).

Decide on your priority and be prepared to exclude any items that conflict with it. If you want to have a pond in the garden, you will do well to exclude trees from that area, or the falling leaves from the tree will cause difficulties by blowing into the pond and rotting. Ponds need quite a lot of maintenance, and you should make sure that you are prepared to do all the work before installing one. Nothing is *less* refreshing than a stagnant pond covered with green weed, although a well-kept pool is a great pleasure.

Paths, walls and steps are often a major item in making a garden, and should be planned with even more care than the flower beds, because they are harder to change afterwards. So make sure that you site all the permanent items very accurately. Paths and steps must always be built with safety in mind: remember that you are legally responsible for the damage if anyone slips and falls while in your garden. If there are elderly people or young children in the family make sure that the pond is safely fenced off.

Basic earth

Digging improves the soil in many ways, especially on a new site, or where the earth is heavy and wet. Ideally the garden should be dug over before winter to enable the frost to break up the soil. The action of frost and wind improves drainage and dries out heavy clay soils. Air can get to the lower layers, making the soil warmer for spring growing. Organic matter decay is also speeded up. The rewards of this hard labour will easily be seen when plants begin to grow in the warmer weather.

Digging can be done in two ways: single and double digging. Single-digging is 1 spit (1 spade blade) deep, and double-digging twice as deep. The basic method for both is the same. Make a trench 1 spit wide and remove the soil from this trench to the end of the plot. Dig a second trench, turning the soil over into the bottom of the first trench, making sure that the vegetation is well covered. Repeat this process, putting the soil from the third trench into the second trench. Finally, when the area is fully dug over, the soil removed from the first trench can go into the last one. Double-digging varies only in that, when the first layer of soil is removed from a trench, the heavy subsoil at the bottom is forked over 1 spit deeper and compost can be added. Always keep the spade blade vertical and dig sections about 6 in (15 cm) wide by 1 spit deep at a time. It is useful to mark out the trenches with string.

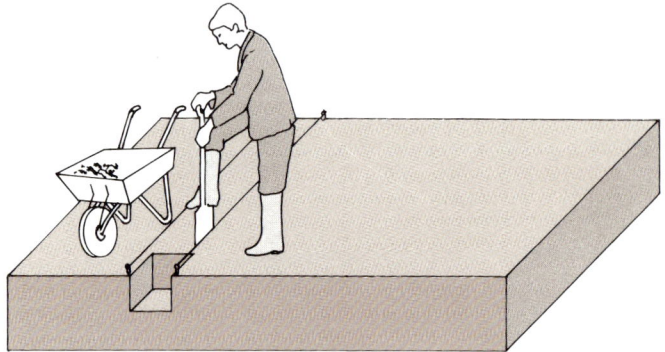

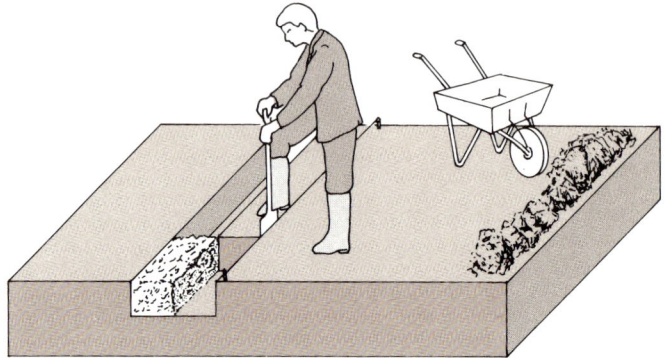

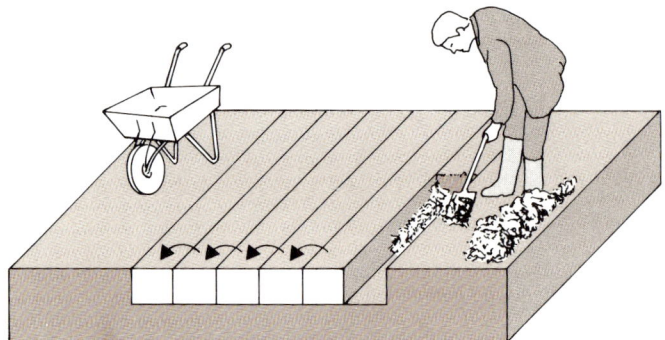

Soil is made up of two types of material, mineral and organic, and supports a 'soil population' of creatures ranging from earthworms to micro-organisms. Fertility depends on the proportions of each of these elements in the soil. Many plants have specific soil needs and it is important to establish which type of soil you have for success in growing. You can also adapt your soil to encourage its best qualities. The table below shows you how to identify your soil and how to treat it.

Sand
Sandy soil is never sticky and will not form a ball in your hand. It is light and dries quickly, needing water badly in the summer. Sand loses nutrients quickly – it is a 'hungry soil', so the best treatment is with lots of compost, manure and fertilizer. It is a warm soil, so spring crops do well if organic matter is present.

Clay
Clay will not change shape when rolled in your hand. It is heavy to work, gets waterlogged in the winter and dries hard in the summer. Clay soil is too cold for early crops. The best remedies are good drainage, double-digging in early winter and lime dressings. Compost and manure can also be added.

Loam
Loam is a dark soil which easily forms a ball in your hand but crumbles if pressed firmly. It has the best qualities of sand and clay and is the ideal gardening soil. Loam needs no treatment, but maintain its condition with dressings of lime and fertilizers.

Chalk
Chalky soil is easily identified by noticing the white subsoil. It is sticky when wet, but drains freely like sand and is bad for vegetables. Treat as for sandy soil, but do not dig over deeply. It is rich in lime, so certain plants which hate lime, eg rhododendrons, do badly in it.

Peat
Peat is recognized by the near blackness of its colour, and by its spongy texture. It is acid and poor for growing although it is very rich in organic material. You can dramatically improve this soil by drainage, adding lime and digging in loam topsoil.

Stony
Stony soil is usually rather infertile, as it does not retain water. It is impossible to clear all the stones away, so the best approach is to try to add to its nutrients by digging in plenty of compost, manure and fertilizers.

These six classifications cover most of the main soil types. If your soil does not fit neatly into one of these categories, treat it the same as the one it most closely resembles. Soil types are not absolute, but shade off into different combinations.

Drainage

Drainage is a major problem in heavy soil. The growth of rushes or mosses indicates poor drainage. Causes of this are an impervious layer beneath the topsoil (which is cured by double-digging), clay soil (improved by lime, gypsum or peat dressings), or deep layers that hold water (treated by making drains in a herring bone pattern). This is hard work, but should be one of the first garden chores you do, if your soil is wet.

Herring bone method
Water runs downhill, so dig the main channel from the highest to the lowest point in the garden. Then dig side trenches 18 in (45 cm) deep and 15 ft (5 m) apart to run into the main drain. These should be staggered where they meet the main channel. The water will run to the lowest point of the garden, where there must be a ditch or a soakaway to accommodate it.

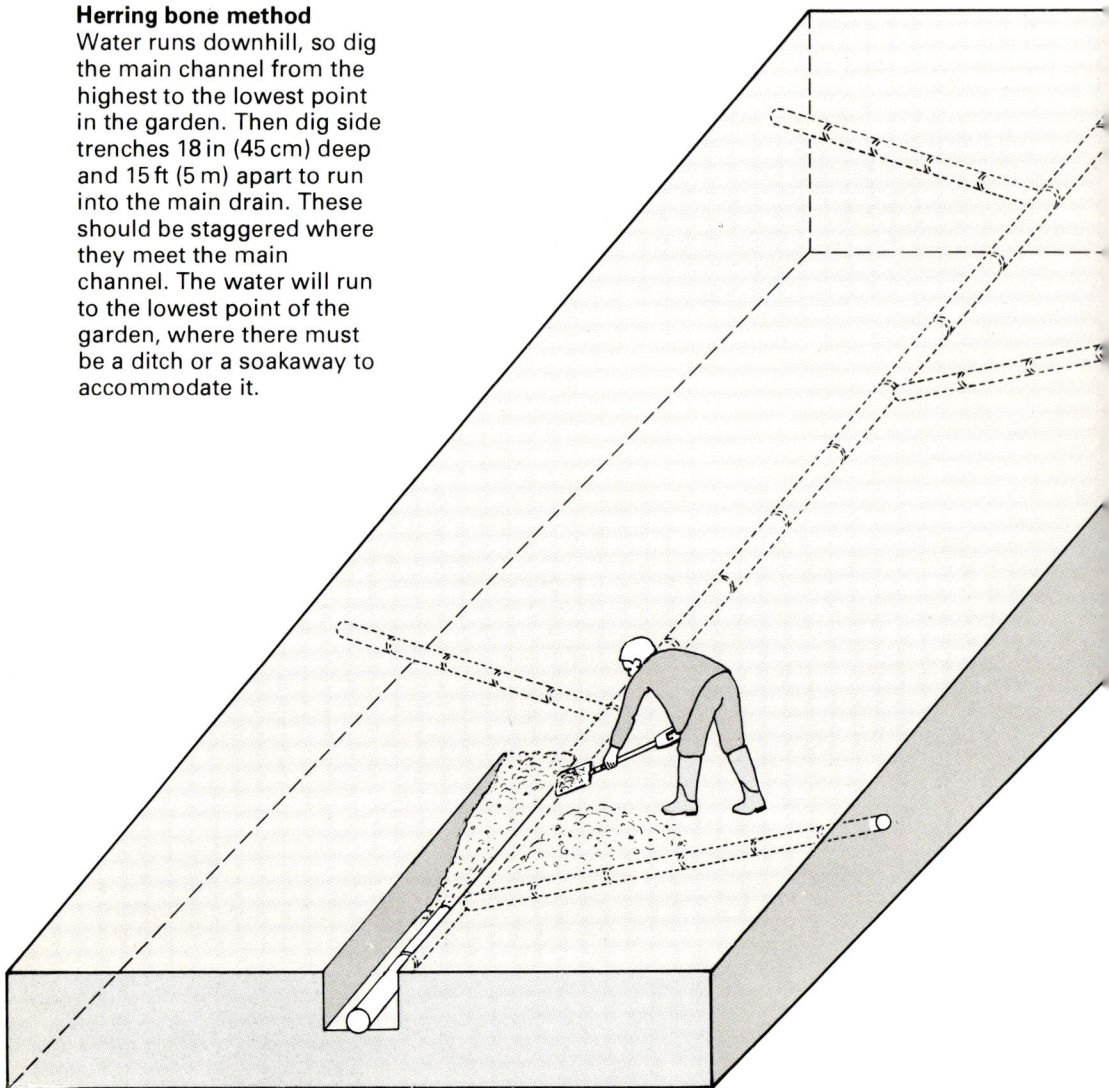

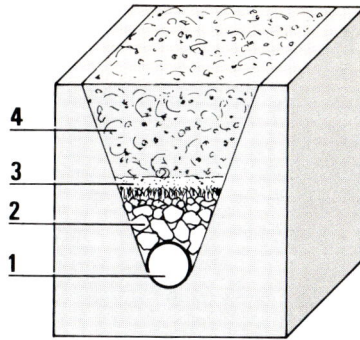

Pipe drains

1 Use earthenware pipes 3–4 in (7–9 cm) diameter for main drains, 2–3 in (5–7 cm) diameter for side drains.
2 Cover with 3 in (7 cm) of stones, and **3** a layer of inverted turf to stop soil washing in. **4** Replace the topsoil.

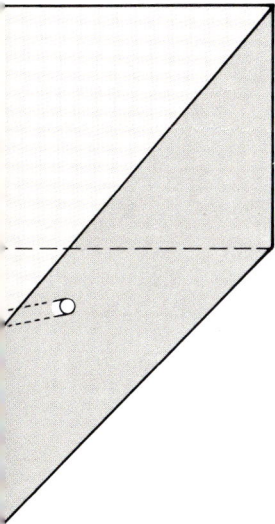

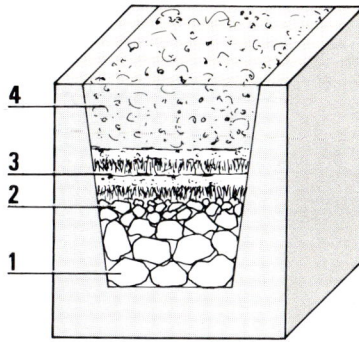

Rubble drains

These use the same principle as soakaways.
1 Place large stones on the bottom, **2** small stones on top. These should be loosely packed. **3** Cover with a double layer of inverted turf to prevent stones mixing with soil.
4 Replace topsoil.

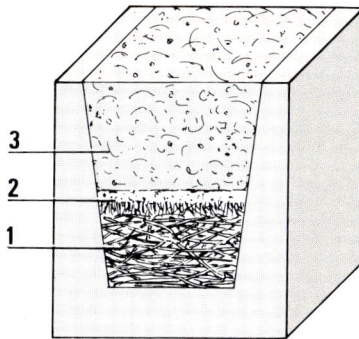

Brushwood drains

This is an old drainage method, which can be effective for many years.
1 Lay willow branches at the base of the trench.
2 Cover with inverted turf and **3** replace the topsoil.

Soakaway or sump drain

This is a large pit, about 3 ft (1 m) deeper than the deepest drain and at least 4 ft (1.3 m) square. The pit is left open until you see whether it is big enough to hold all the water it must cope with; if not, you must dig a bigger hole. When you are sure it is big enough, fill the hole with loose rubble, and cover this with turf, then with soil.

Adding to the earth

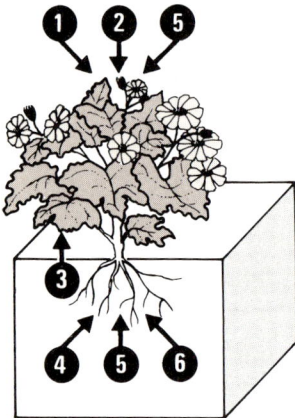

Diagram showing cycle of plant requirements
Nitrogen is needed for growth, phosphorus for healthy roots, and potassium, for fruit development and hardy plants.
1 CO_2 from air
2 Energy from sun is used to make plant sugar
3 If the plant is removed, soil loses nutrients
4 Major nutrients: nitrogen, phosphorus, potassium, calcium, magnesium, sulphur
5 Water
6 Trace elements: boron, copper, iron, manganese, molybdenum, zinc

Successful growing depends on the amount of nutrients present in the soil. All soils can be improved or maintained by adding plant food in the form of fertilizers or organic matter (manure and compost), and by correcting levels of acidity with lime dressings.

Fertilizers replace nutrients lost from the soil in weathering and cropping. Plants need many nutrients, but only nitrogen, phosphorus and potassium are removed in large enough quantities to need to be added in fertilizer. The rest can be maintained by keeping a high level of organic matter in the soil. Rake in top dressings in the spring carefully, without scattering onto the leaves of the young plants. Autumn is the time to apply base dressings, so that soil is enriched before planting. Store all fertilizers in a dry place away from children.

Manure can be obtained from stables or farms and provides organic matter or humus that both improves the physical properties of the soil and helps to retain its nutrients. Animal

FERTILIZER	NUTRIENT	ORIGIN
Dried Blood	nitrogen	organic
Hoof and horn meal	nitrogen	organic
Nitro-chalk	nitrogen	inorganic
Sulphate of ammonia	nitrogen	inorganic
Bone meal	phosphorus	organic
Superphosphate	phosphorus	inorganic
Basic slag	phosphorus	inorganic
Sulphate of potash	potassium	inorganic
Compound	nitrogen phosphorus potassium	inorganic

manure is the best to use and can be from horses, cows or pigs. Fresh manure should be covered with soil and allowed to rot before digging in several months before planting. There may be a slight risk of tetanus or salmonella if manure is not used hygienically, so wash your hands carefully after applying manure and keep children away.

Other sources of organic matter include: sewage sludge, spent mushroom compost, spent hops, seaweed, leaf mould, peat, sawdust and poultry manure (a top dressing). These are generally less successful to use than farmyard manure, and may be expensive.

Lime is easily washed out of the soil, which leaves the soil with a high level of acidity. Lime contains calcium, helps to break up heavy soils and keeps some pests away. Apply lime dressings in the autumn (but not with manure or compost), after first testing the soil for acidity: too much lime also causes problems.

A new dustbin is very useful in the toolshed for storing potting compost, sand or some kinds of fertilizer.

Which fertilizer you choose depends on the nature of the soil, the kind of plants you want in your garden, and the price you can afford to pay. The correct fertilizer for the job, applied in the right place at the right time, will make all the difference to your results.

DRESSING	WHEN TO APPLY	PER SQ YD (SQ M)	COMMENTS
top	spring	1–2 oz (30–60 g)	Use on pot plants, lettuce. Expensive.
base	autumn	4 oz (130 g)	Expensive.
top	spring	½–1 oz (15–30 g)	Quick-acting and long-lasting. Suitable for most soils. Cheap.
top	spring	1 oz (30 g)	Use on green vegetables. Cheap. Corrosive: store in dry area.
base	autumn	2–4 oz (65–130 g)	Use on all green vegetables and for trees and shrubs.
top	spring	1–2 oz (30–60 g)	Use on young plants, especially green vegetables.
top	spring	1–2 oz (30–60 g)	Helps reduce acidity.
top	spring	2 oz (60 g)	Most widely available potassium fertilizer. Use for fruit trees.
top	spring	4 oz (130 g)	May be sufficient for ordinary gardener. Use on roses, lawns.

Levelling ground

Many gardens have sloping areas and these will vary a great deal in gradient. It is not always desirable to level a garden completely. If the garden is small, gentle slopes will add to the spatial interest. Severe slopes can be a problem, causing difficulties of drainage (page 24) and maintenance, as water runs off the higher areas, leaving them dry, and accumulates in soggy hollows. Lawns are easier to cut and care for if they are fairly level. An alternative to levelling is terracing: retaining walls are useful here.

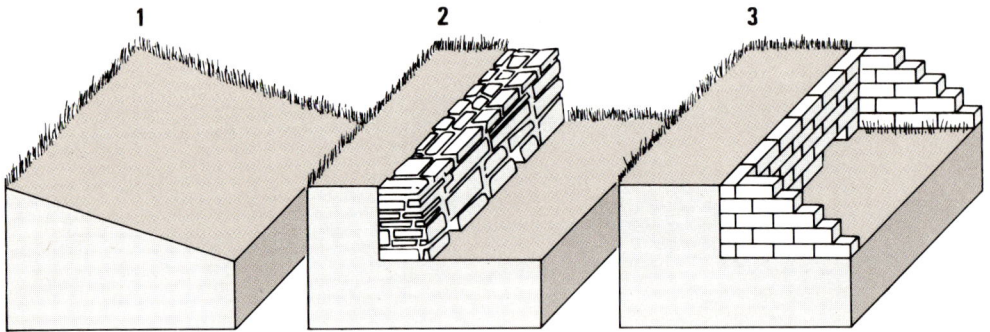

A slope can be grassed over, but must be gentle enough to allow a lawn-mower to be used safely. Otherwise, it can be terraced, with a flat surface and a retaining wall: the wall can be either a drystone wall or a brick one with buttresses. But the wall must allow for adequate drainage of the soil behind it.

1 Grassy slope
2 Sloping drystone wall
3 Brick wall with buttresses

Below: gardens can be landscaped to accommodate changes in level, and such a garden can be much more interesting than one that is completely flat.
1 Lawn
2 Path
3 Drystone wall with plants
4 Flower bed
5 Retaining wall

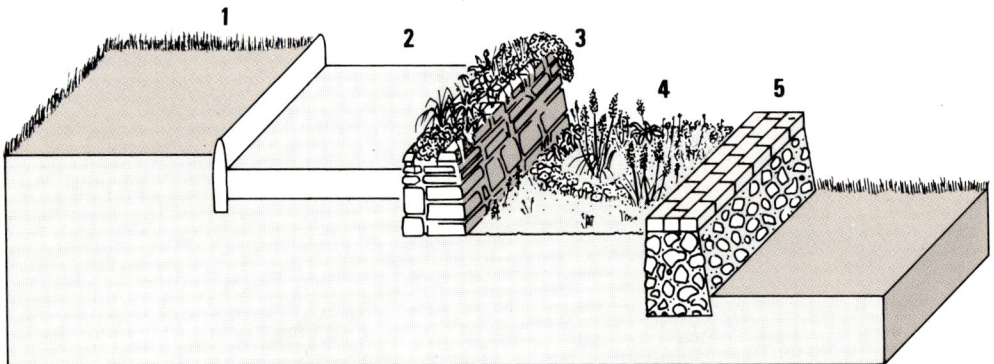

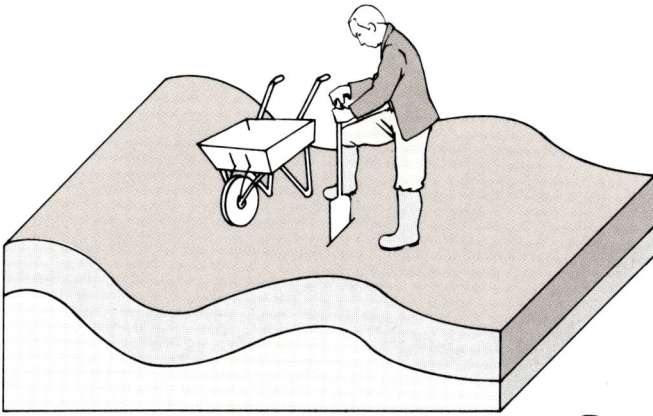

Many changes in the garden involve moving soil. When this is necessary try to use the soil to create another feature, eg a mound. When levelling, topsoil must not be buried; plants will not grow well on the subsoil.

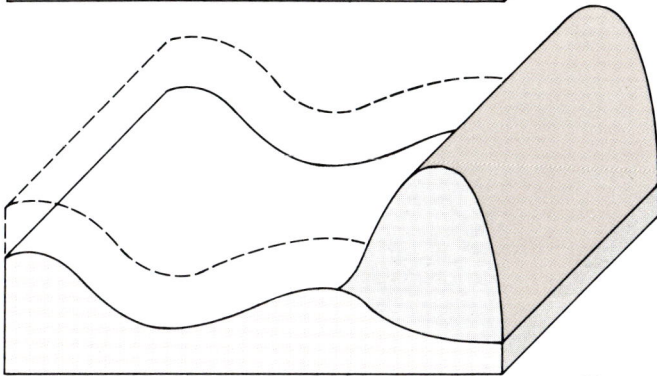

Move the topsoil (top 16 in/40 cm of soil) to the lower end of the garden. In new gardens, if the topsoil is buried under rubble, clear this first.

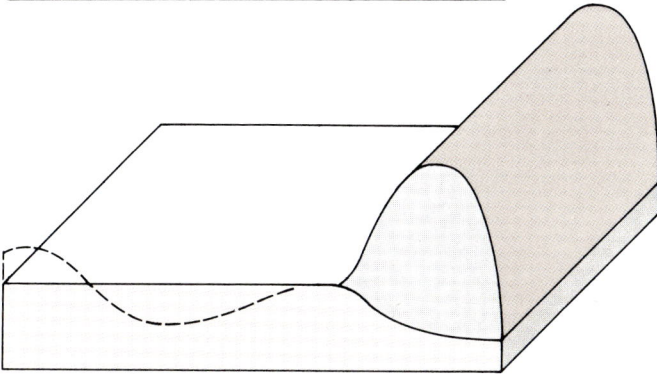

Level the subsoil.

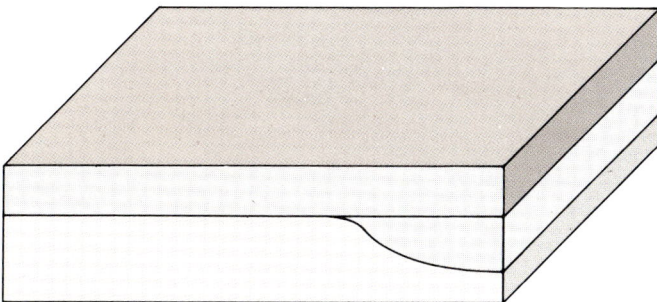

Replace topsoil on levelled area.

Surfaces

A change in texture or surface level is an easy way to create variety. Many of these changes could arise out of specific requirements for utility areas or playing areas for children. Apart from these practical needs, some of the ideas shown below have the added advantage of giving interest in the winter months, when there are few flowers to provide colour in the garden. Try not to combine too many different ideas in one design. Consider the overall picture and aim to keep all the component elements compatible.

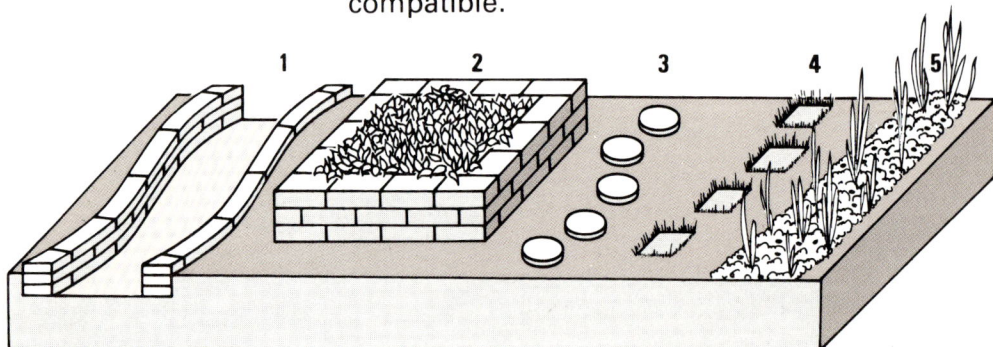

Changes in level (above)
1 Sunken path
2 Raised flower bed giving easy access for older people
3 Raised stepping stones
4 Lowered stepping stones
5 Low ground cover combined with tall grasses

Colour and texture (below)
Flowers traditionally provide colour in gardens, but subtle effects can be achieved with the use of contrasting textures and materials.

1 Gravel
2 Pebbles
3 Grass
4 Sand
5 Water
6 Mosses
7 Stones and grass
8 Flowers

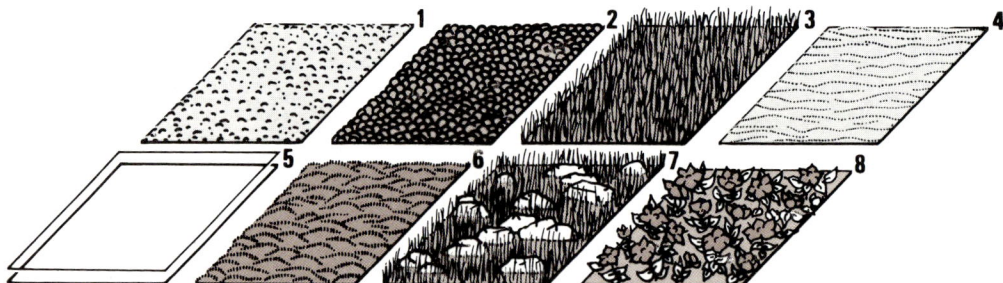

Style

A natural country garden has softer boundaries and is the perfect place for rockeries, informal shrubs and wild grasses.
In a formal garden, hedges should be clipped and lawns edged; flower beds look best in a geometric design.

Hedges were formerly condemned for harbouring garden pests; but they also encourage the birds that get rid of those insects for the gardener. And who would want a garden without any birds in it?

Focal point

A central garden feature such as an elaborate flower bed or a monkey puzzle tree can give a larger garden a sense of unity. One of the secrets of garden design is to choose the right size for the central feature; a large garden needs a really grand and striking centre, whereas in a small garden a very large tree or an elaborate central flower bed would be overpowering. On a smaller scale, a statue or a garden seat makes an excellent focus.

Changing viewpoint

A change of scenery is good for everyone, and this garden is completely different when seen from opposite viewpoints. From the house, the garden looks very informal. The lawn is irregular in shape, and so is the 'natural' pool, which is fed from the unseen formal pool by a circulating pump. The wall behind the pool is faced with uneven rock, and this hides the formal part of the pool from the house. The nearby trees are loosely spreading in shape.

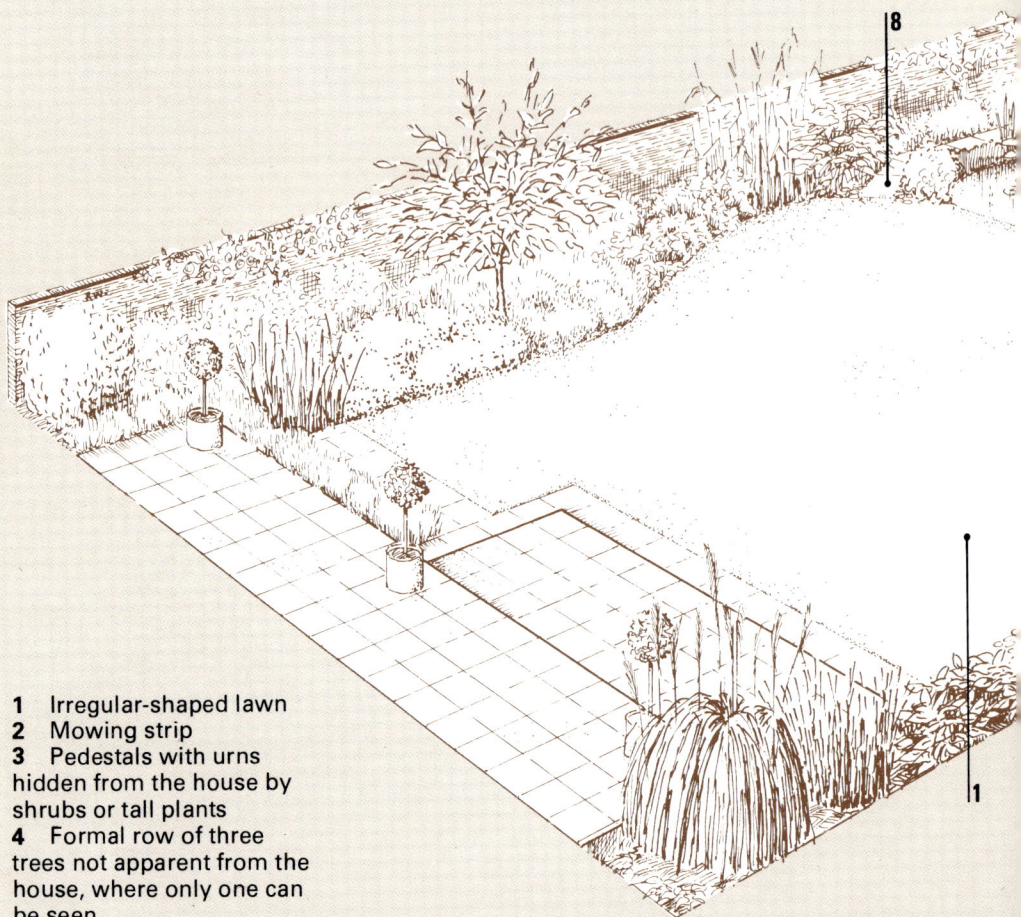

8

1

1 Irregular-shaped lawn
2 Mowing strip
3 Pedestals with urns hidden from the house by shrubs or tall plants
4 Formal row of three trees not apparent from the house, where only one can be seen

This is an oblique view of the garden, from an upstairs window next door; some of the formal touches can be seen here, but would be hidden from the house whose garden it is. On the next pages you can see the view from the far end of the garden, back towards the house.

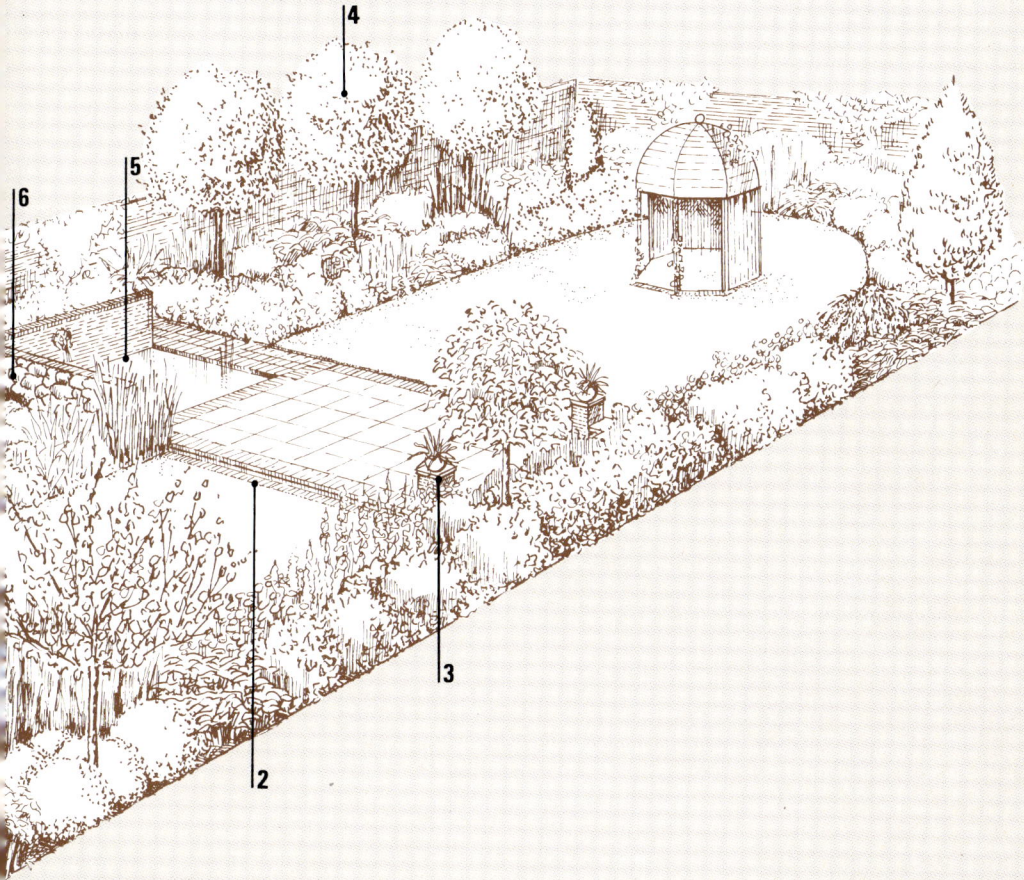

5 Formal square pool hidden from the house by the low wall
6 Rock-faced wall behind informal pool, covering the formal brickwork, which would be out of place here with the irregular pool
7 Small willow such as Salix purpurea 'Pendula' or Salix caprea 'Pendula' will not outgrow the setting
8 Hidden path giving access to pools and border for maintenance

01

This is a view of the same garden as that on the
previous pages, but seen this time looking
towards the house. From this end, the more
formal aspects of the garden are predominant.
The lawns are all square or circular. The shape
of the house itself contributes to the formality,
as do the two bay trees (there are actually three,
but one is unseen from here) flanking the door.
The part of the pool seen from this side is
square, with a central fountain, and backed by a
rectangular brick wall. The geometrical

The gardens pictured in
this book are all mature.
If your handiwork does
not quite satisfy you at
first, it may be because it
is still new. Plants and
trees need time to settle
in and grow, and new
paving needs to be
weathered. So give your
garden time to mellow.

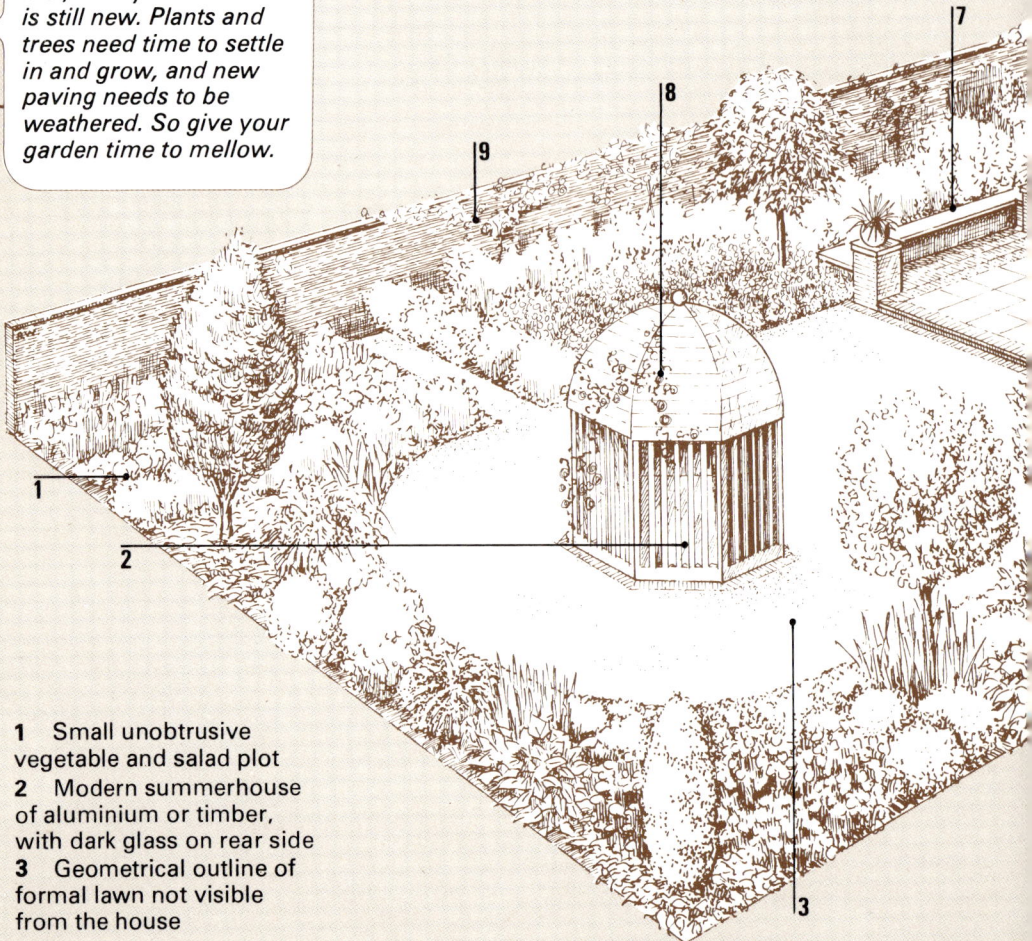

1 Small unobtrusive
vegetable and salad plot
2 Modern summerhouse
of aluminium or timber,
with dark glass on rear side
3 Geometrical outline of
formal lawn not visible
from the house

summerhouse also emphasises the formality of this view, as does the orderly row of round trees and the seat flanked by two pedestals with urns. Behind the summerhouse, and thus hidden from either of the usual viewpoints, is a small but useful plot for vegetables and salad.

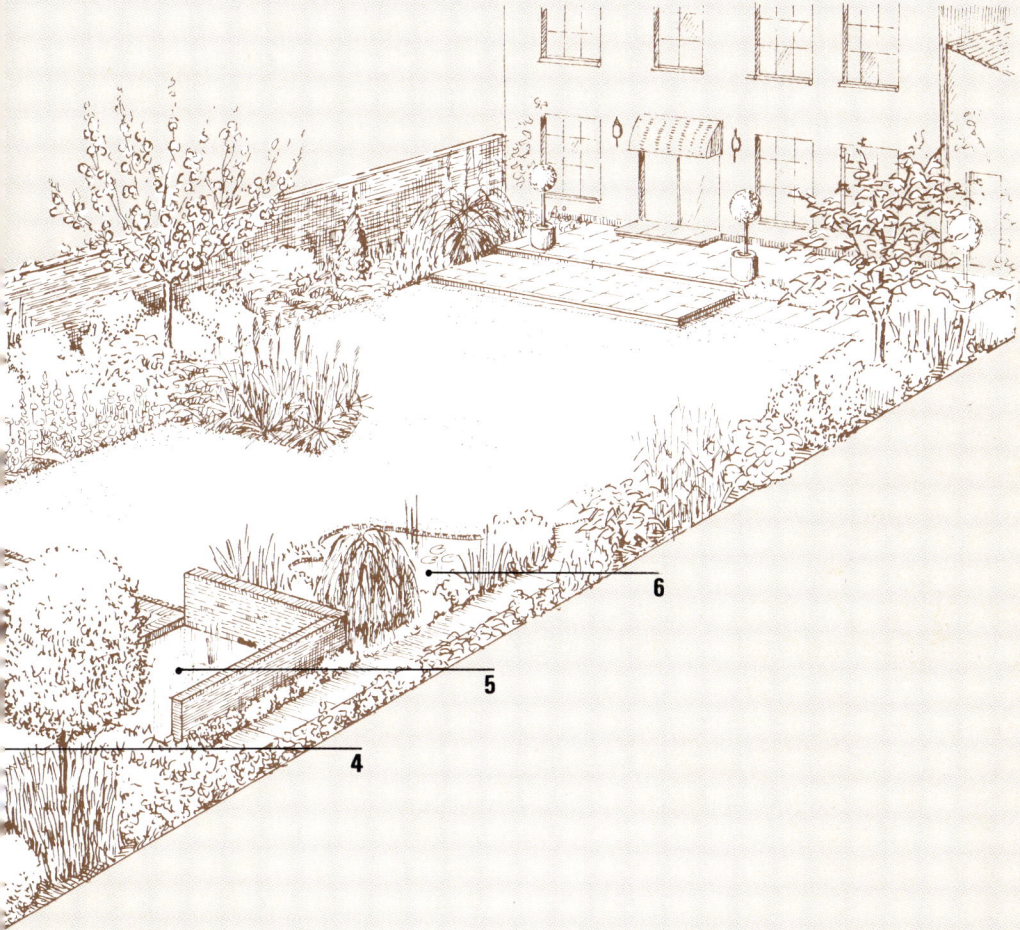

4 Naturally mop-headed trees include Robinia pseudoacacia 'Inermis'
5 Formal pool visible from summerhouse (not from house)
6 Informal pool now hidden from summerhouse

7 Seat flanked by two urns planted with shrubs
8 Climbing roses over the roof of the summerhouse
9 Shrubs trained to grow along the wall, disguising the hard line

Changing character

The garden on these pages and the one on pages 38–9 are on an identical site, but they are completely different in atmosphere. In a street of identical houses, the gardens differ widely, and each reflects the tastes of its owner. It is fairly common for a corner house garden to be triangular in shape, and the problems are different from those of a rectangular plot. The garden on this page is very formal in design, and must be kept very neat and tidy, because any irregularities will show up more. The lawn

1   Wall with brick capping
2   Brick edging to lawn
3   Matching pair of conifers
4   Paved sitting area
5   Flower beds
6   Holly tree
7   Timber pergola
8   Bust on plinth as focal point of whole garden
9   Tree to form background to bust and plinth
10   Path to paved utility area hidden behind tree
11   Large conifer
12   Lavender hedge around lawn
13   Yew, abutus or thorn can be clipped to a ball shape, but some varieties have this shape naturally, eg Robinia pseudoacacia 'Inermis'

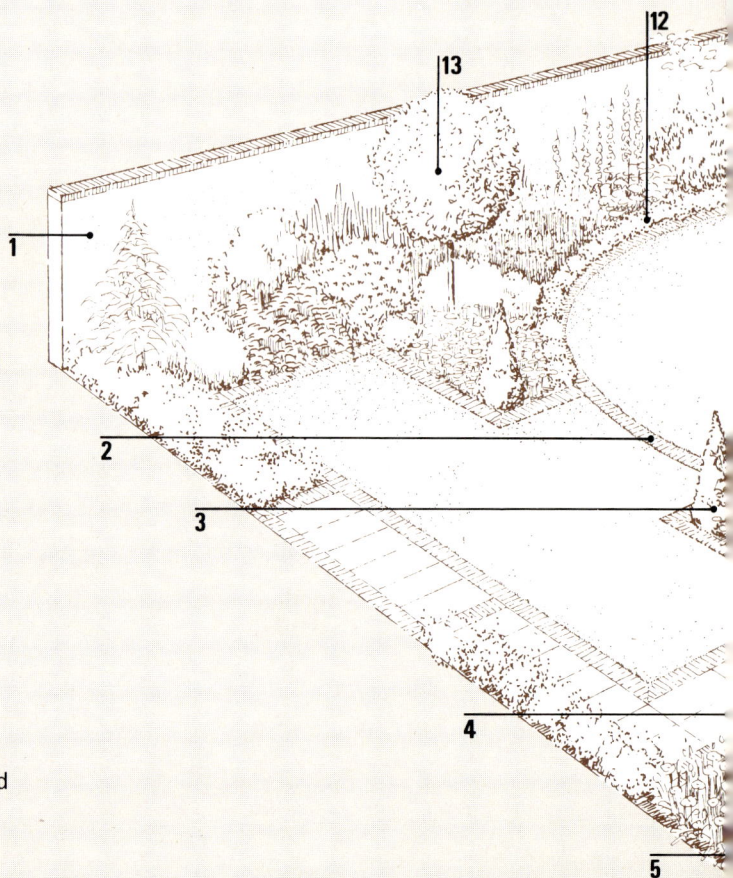

must be cut as soon as it needs trimming, and
the edges neatly tended (pages 80–3). On the
other hand, the quite large paved area will need
no upkeep, and the shrubs and trees can be
chosen so as to be trouble-free too (pages 84–7
and 137).

A pergola is useful in a
very new garden, as it is
quickly made and soon
covered with plants, thus
giving a change of height
long before a tree could
grow to any size.

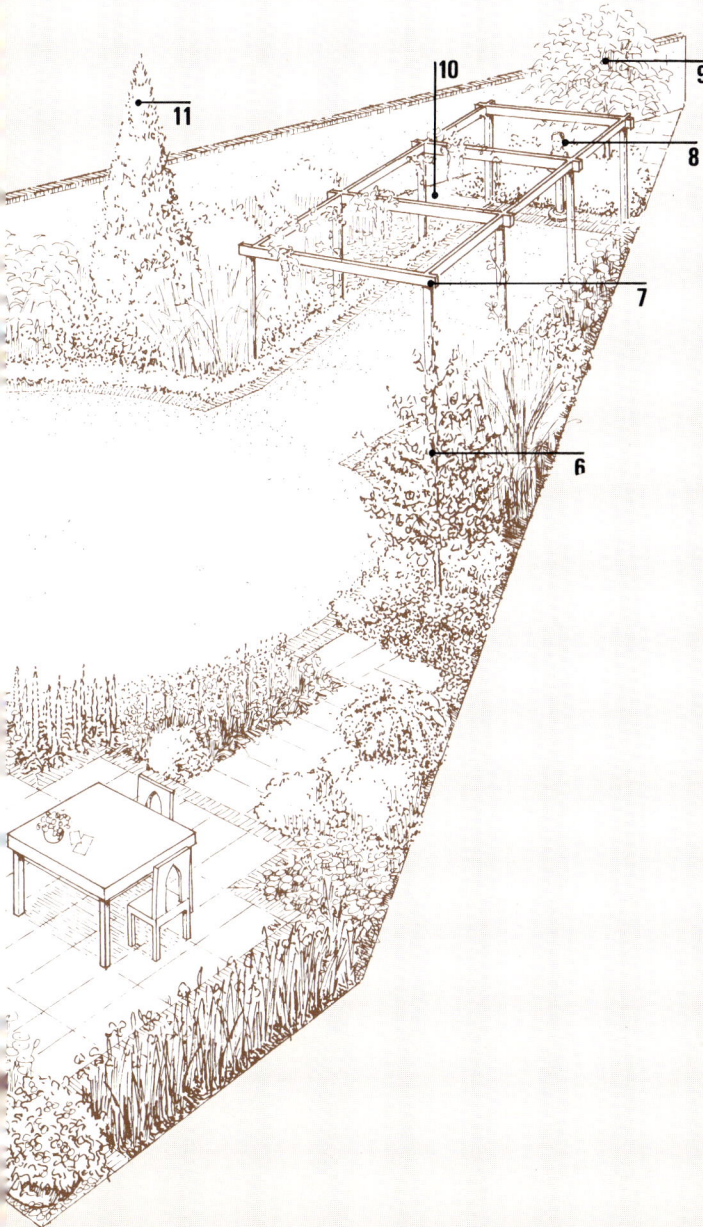

11

10

9

8

7

6

This garden is carefully
designed to give a feeling
of peace and order. The
brick edging around the
lawn matches the brick
capping on the wall, and
also continues into the
paved sitting area, thus
giving continuity. (It also
makes it easier to mow the
lawn and to maintain the
circular shape exactly.) The
two matching conifers
frame the view from the
house, as do the larger
conifer and its balancing
holly tree further down the
garden. The pergola then
directs attention to the bust
at the focal point of the
whole design.

02

On the same corner site as the garden on the previous two pages, another gardener might choose this completely different layout. This design is rustic and informal, with a rambling path of stepping stones and an irregularly shaped lawn. In a garden whose focal point is a birdbath, it would be a good idea to grow a few berried shrubs that attract birds, such as cotoneaster or pyracantha (see page 84). Thick hedges make a good nesting place for birds.

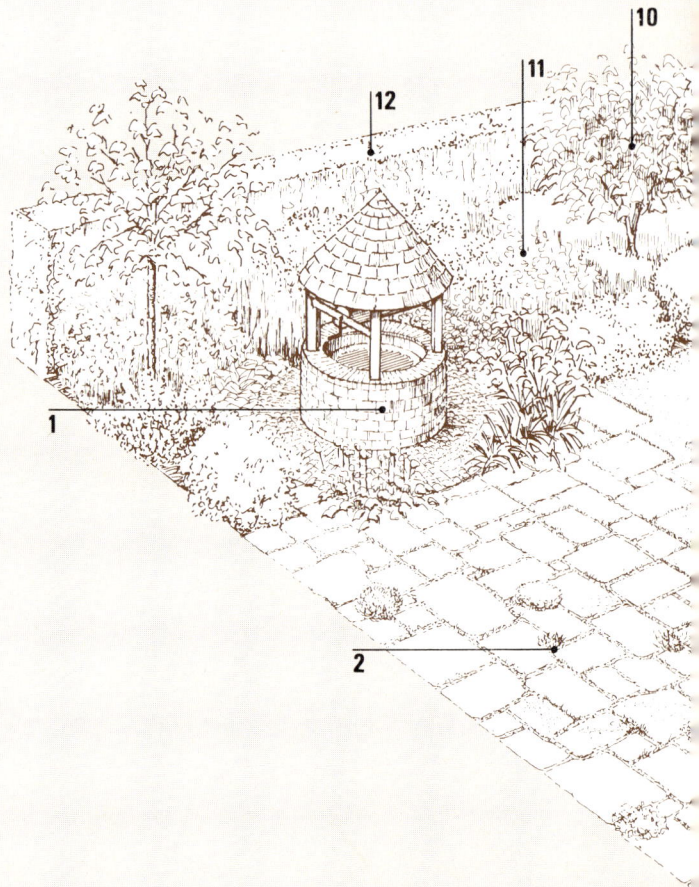

1 Barbecue disguised as rustic well
2 Paving with some plants in cracks between stones, eg Thymus coccineus, Pratia angulata 'Treadwellii', Potentilla verna nana or aubretia
3 Shed disguised by plants and pergola
4 Bench seat
5 Stepping stone path
6 *Small* weeping tree (see page 33)
7 Birdbath as focal point
8 Simple timber trellis
9 Lawn
10 Trees give height
11 Mixed shrubs and flowers
12 Hedge

And the birds may repay your hospitality by eating vast numbers of caterpillars, slugs, snails and aphids, which would otherwise spoil your plants. Disguise your garden shed, and hide away the working areas: a compost heap is extremely useful, but no one could call it decorative.

Hedges make great demands on the soil, and their roots spread a long way around. It is unrealistic to plant flower borders close up against a hedge and expect them to do well.

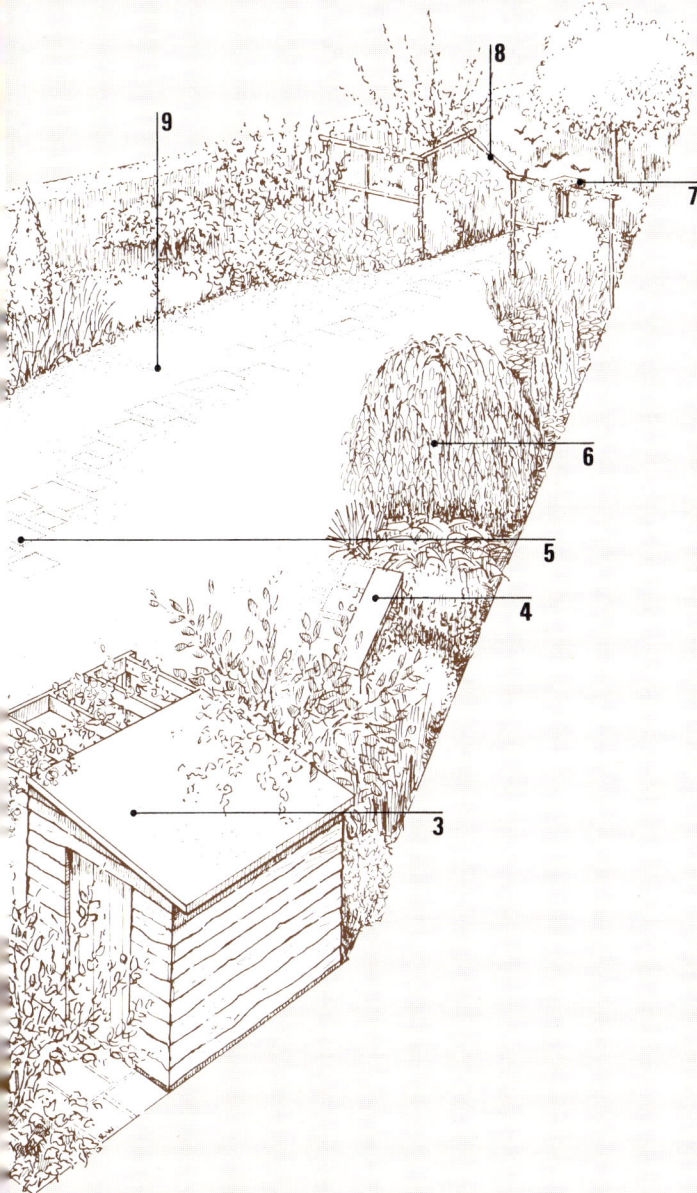

There are a few cunning ideas in this garden to make life easier for the gardener. The stepping stones that form a path across the lawn are set so that they are slightly below the level of the grass surface, to make mowing the lawn easier. And a hidden path gives the gardener access to the hedge when it needs trimming. A tiny pergola built on the front of the garden shed and covered with a climbing rose helps to disguise the building, which is thus handy to the house but not unsightly from the window.

03

Chapter two
Location of gardens

There are five designs in this chapter and they deal specifically with the problem of location. Although location is the basic theme, all the designs incorporate ideas on how to reduce maintenance and how to provide variety and interest at a reasonable cost, and also include provisions for different recreational and work areas. It is not necessary to treat these plans as blueprints for your garden. There will be differences of size, and specific requirements of your own which would probably make this impossible. The gardens shown are somewhat larger than average.

The chapter includes a country garden, front and back gardens in a suburban area, a roof garden, and a design to solve special problems of location caused by external features. Each example works by showing a view of the site, with a list of the elements in the plan. The following pages give a description of particular features, showing how they solve various problems and meet the requirements of each situation.

A Victorian photograph of a quiet London suburban garden.

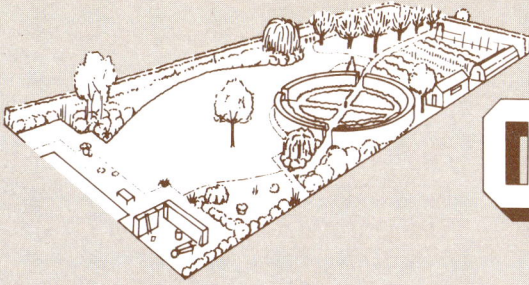

04 A large country garden can accommodate several much smaller gardens within it.

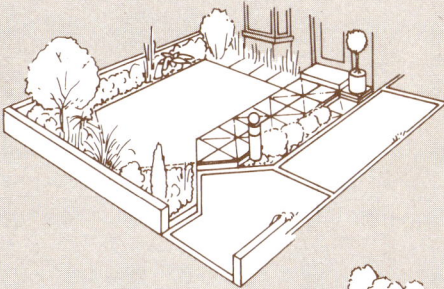

05 A suburban front garden must efficiently welcome both cars and visitors.

06 A suburban back garden, if well laid out, need not seem boringly rectangular.

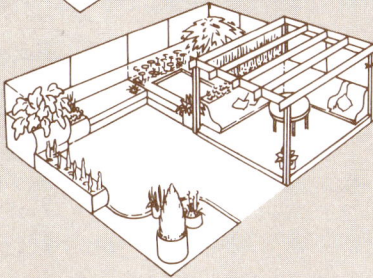

07 A roof garden may be a city dweller's only taste of fresh air and greenery.

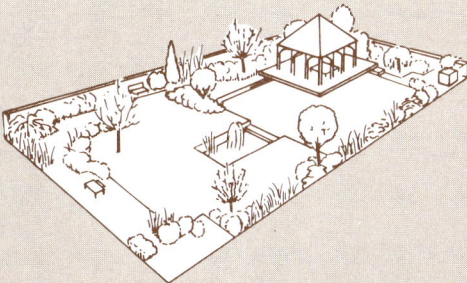

08 An overlooked garden can nonetheless have many peaceful secluded corners.

A country garden

In a country garden, size presents the problem of maintenance. The best solution is often to create a number of different areas which vary in the care they require and provide for a range of activities. Advantage should be taken of the rural position, by keeping the garden as natural in appearance as possible. The boundary to the garden need not be seen, to allow more conformity with the surrounding countryside. The grass can be longer and the edges less manicured. An effective way of giving the

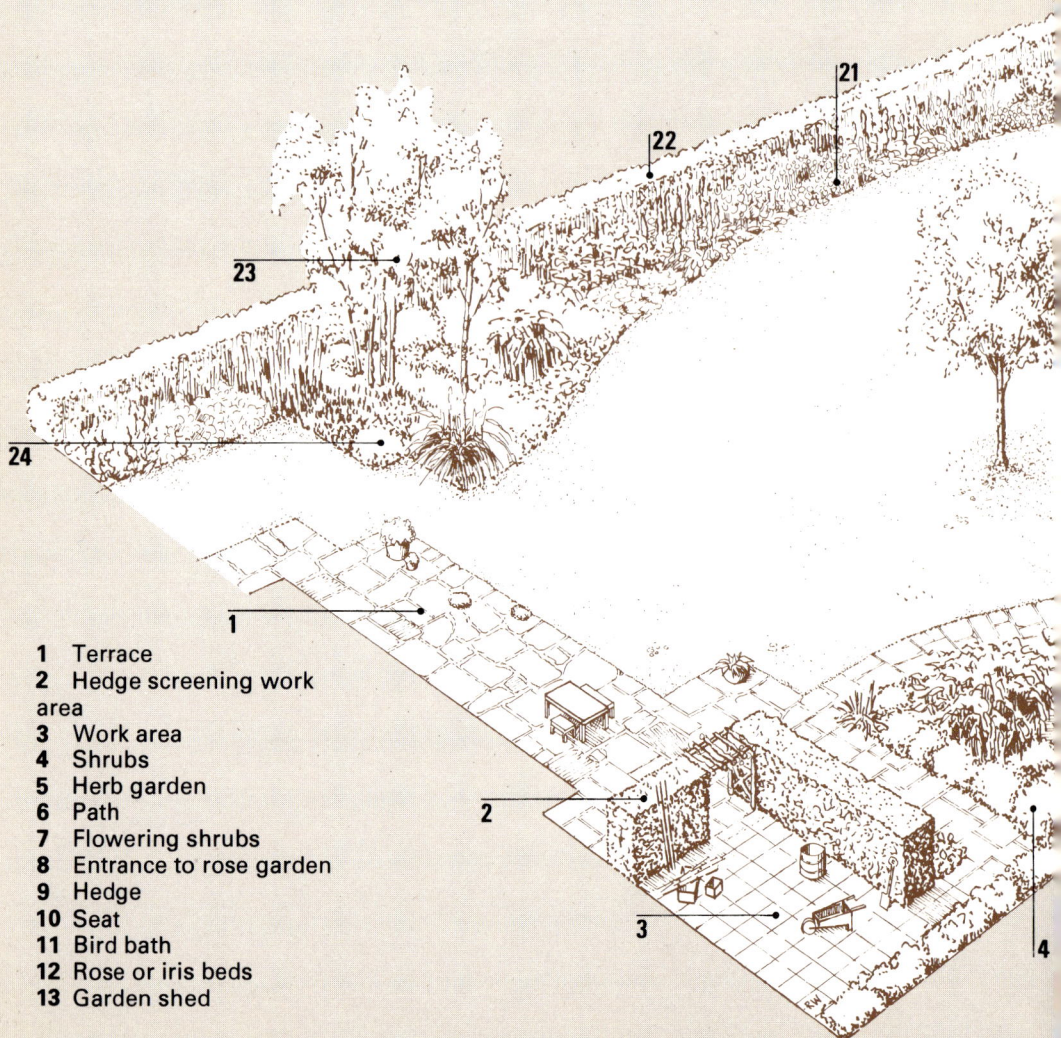

1 Terrace
2 Hedge screening work area
3 Work area
4 Shrubs
5 Herb garden
6 Path
7 Flowering shrubs
8 Entrance to rose garden
9 Hedge
10 Seat
11 Bird bath
12 Rose or iris beds
13 Garden shed

garden an individual character is to use rockeries and paths (pages 92–5) to provide differences in texture, rather than introducing many brightly coloured plants which may not be native to the area. A garden of this size will accommodate ambitious ideas, so plan carefully to achieve a good effect in design and practicality.

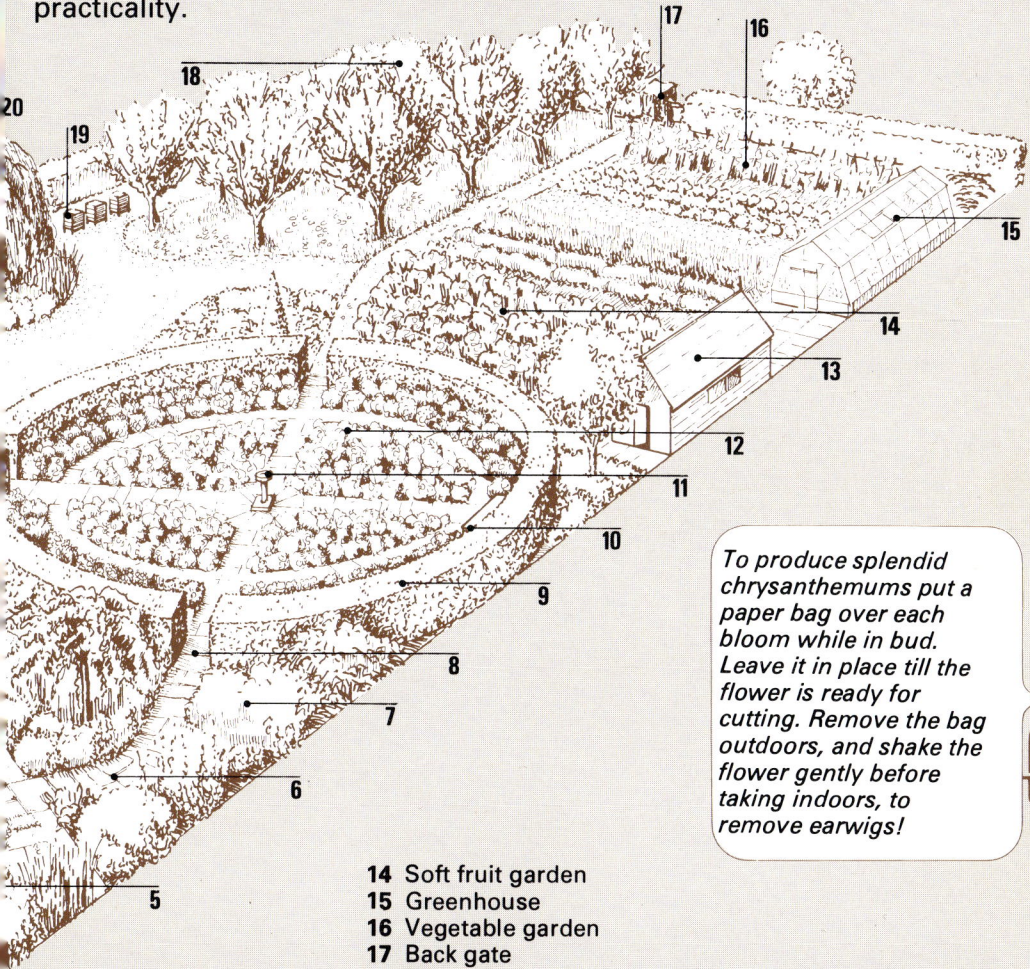

To produce splendid chrysanthemums put a paper bag over each bloom while in bud. Leave it in place till the flower is ready for cutting. Remove the bag outdoors, and shake the flower gently before taking indoors, to remove earwigs!

14 Soft fruit garden
15 Greenhouse
16 Vegetable garden
17 Back gate
18 Orchard
19 Beehives
20 Weeping willow
21 Herbaceous border of old country flowers
22 Countryside hedge of holly, thorn or field maple
23 Group of birches
24 Border of winter flowering shrubs

04

1
Winter shrubs
give colour near to house,
when garden is used less in
bad weather.

2
Birches deliberately inhibit
view of flower border from
this side of the garden.

3
Hedge could contain a fox-
or rabbit-proof fence.

4
Border (page 72) provides
main colour display in
summer, sweeping out to
accommodate willow tree.
Soft lawn edge in keeping
with country setting.

5
In the orchard, the grass
can be allowed to grow
longer, saving on lawn care.
Bulbs may be planted.
Beehives and poultry can
be kept here.

6
Soft-fruit garden will
remain hidden from view
even if caged.

7
Vegetable garden is at a
distance from the house for
aesthetic reasons.

8
Good, hard, clean surface
links shed to greenhouse.

9
Evergreen tree (page 86)
hides the garden shed.

10
Rose garden, hidden by a
clipped or informal hedge,
creates a secluded seating
area whose circular shape
is particularly restful. The
rose garden will not be
visible from the main area;
this is an asset in the winter
when it is less attractive.

11
Single tree (page 86) as
intermediate focal point,
softening hard lines of the
rose garden hedge.

12
Path (page 92) of same
stone as terrace, continuing
around hedge to provide a
working strip from which
the hedge can be clipped.

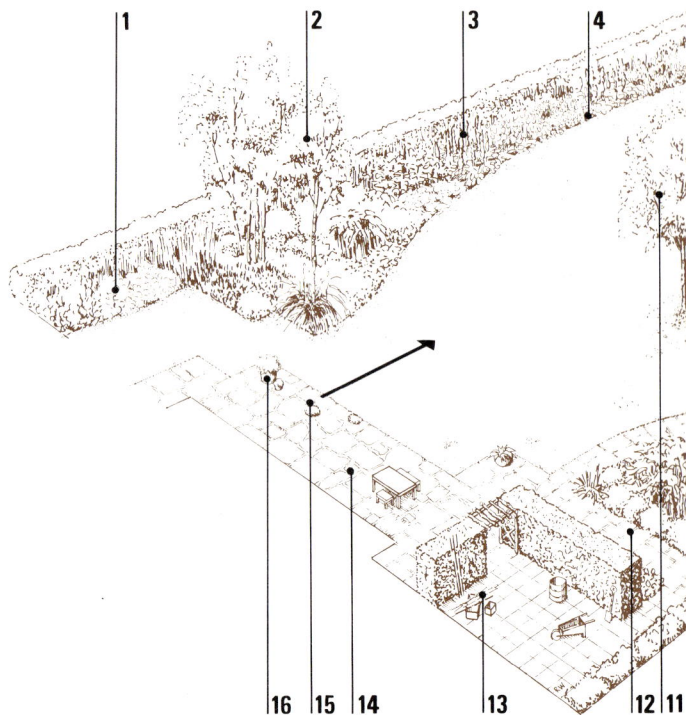

Gardens in a country
location will be more at risk
from predators and pests. It
is worth considering ways
to keep unwelcome visitors
away if they are a nuisance
in the area. Fruit trees may
need to be protected from
birds, and fruit bushes are
best enclosed in a cage if
you want your fair share of
the crop. Some crops may
suffer damage by rabbits.

Foxes are a hazard for any
poultry, and may raid the
dustbins too. Good fences
are essential to keep out
foxes and deer, but the
small animal predators may
be even more difficult to
guard against. On the other
hand, many wild creatures
are of great assistance to
the gardener, keeping down
the insects and mice that
would otherwise plague him.

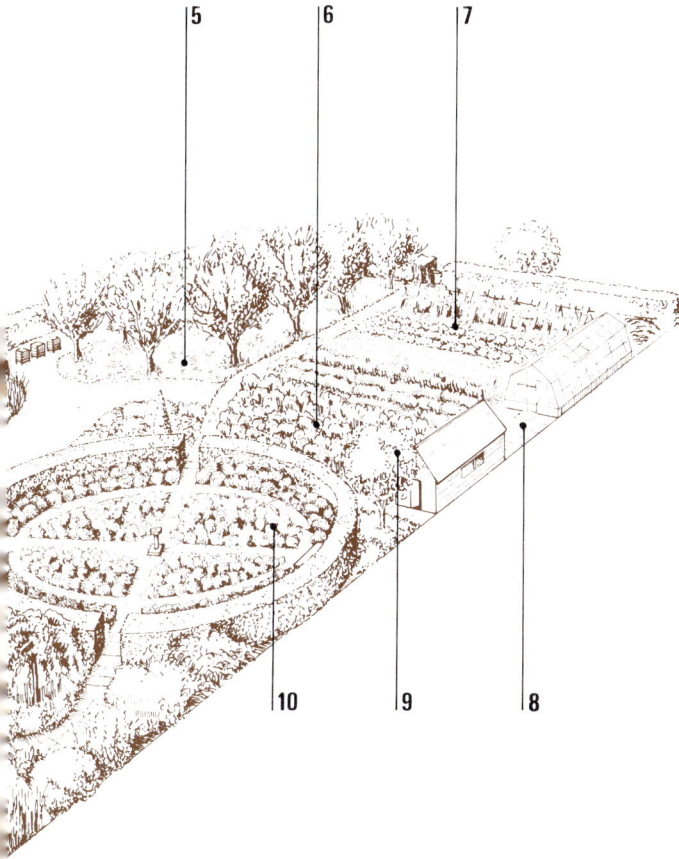

5   6   7

13
Floor of work area in grey
or buff concrete slabs,
which are cheap, easy to
lay, and hygienic. This area
may be left untidy.
14
Terrace (page 59) made of
randomly sized natural
stone, local if possible, or of
good artificial stone. Some
joints left open to allow
moss and carpeting plants
to grow.
15
Main vista looks down the
garden to the open country
beyond.
16
A few herbs planted in
areas left between paving
stones, or in tubs if herbs
grow more freely (eg mint).
Here they are near the
house, easy to reach and
control.

10   9   8

A 1492 illustration shows a
rabbit nibbling the plants.

A front garden

The suburban front garden is usually small and has its own design problems. Ideally it should provide an attractive, welcoming entrance in keeping with the existing style of the house, and give some degree of privacy, while ensuring safe access to the house for those who come and go every day.

These considerations usually mean that it is best to plan a simple design which is easy to maintain, especially if the back garden is large. Simplicity can be achieved by keeping to a

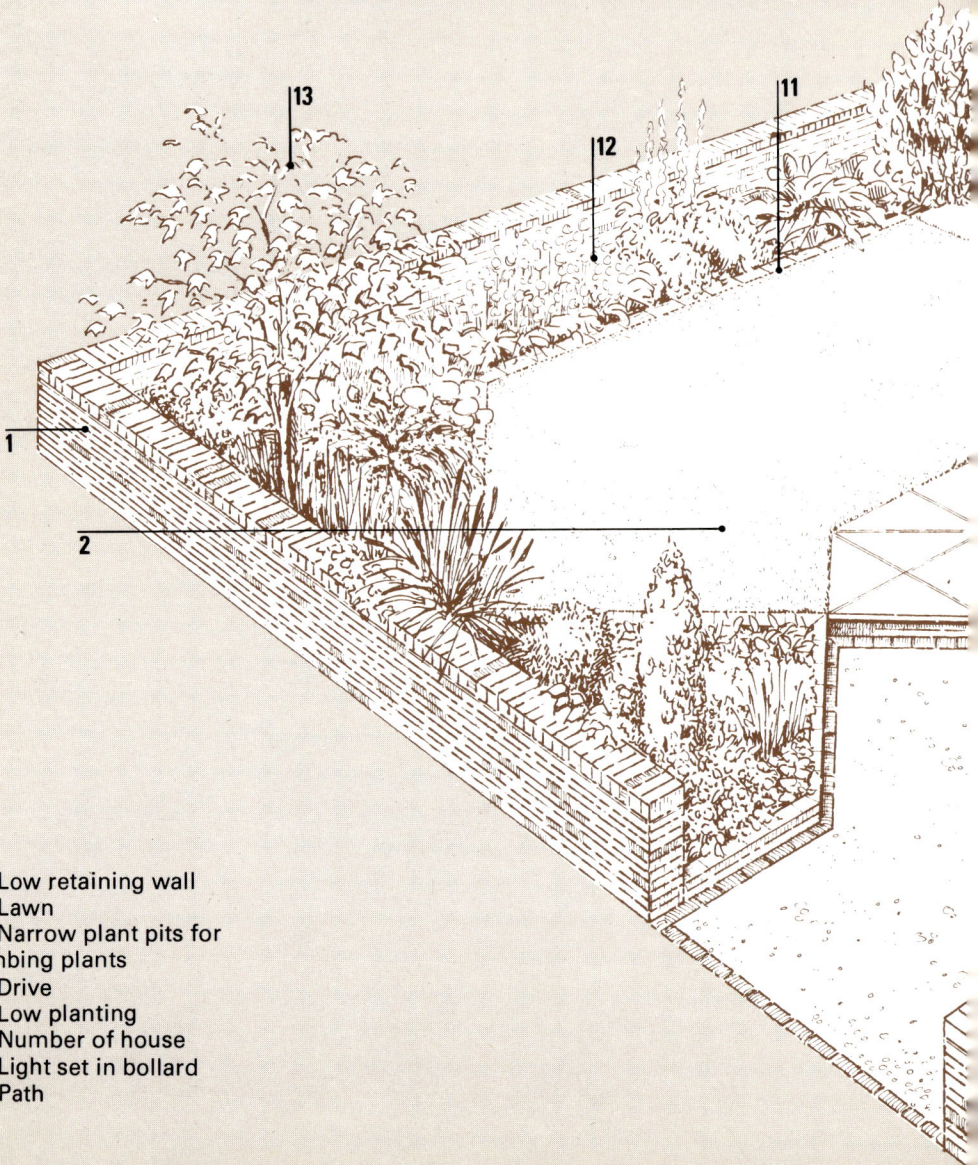

1 Low retaining wall
2 Lawn
3 Narrow plant pits for climbing plants
4 Drive
5 Low planting
6 Number of house
7 Light set in bollard
8 Path

limited range of plants, and by cutting back on the space given to lawns. Trees should be kept to the smaller varieties (page 86). High walls and mature trees will effectively screen out noise and unwelcome sights, but they may obscure the front of the house, ruin any views, and make front rooms dark. They may also prevent a clear view down the drive. It is, however, a good idea to have some type of low retaining wall, fence or hedge, to discourage children and animals.

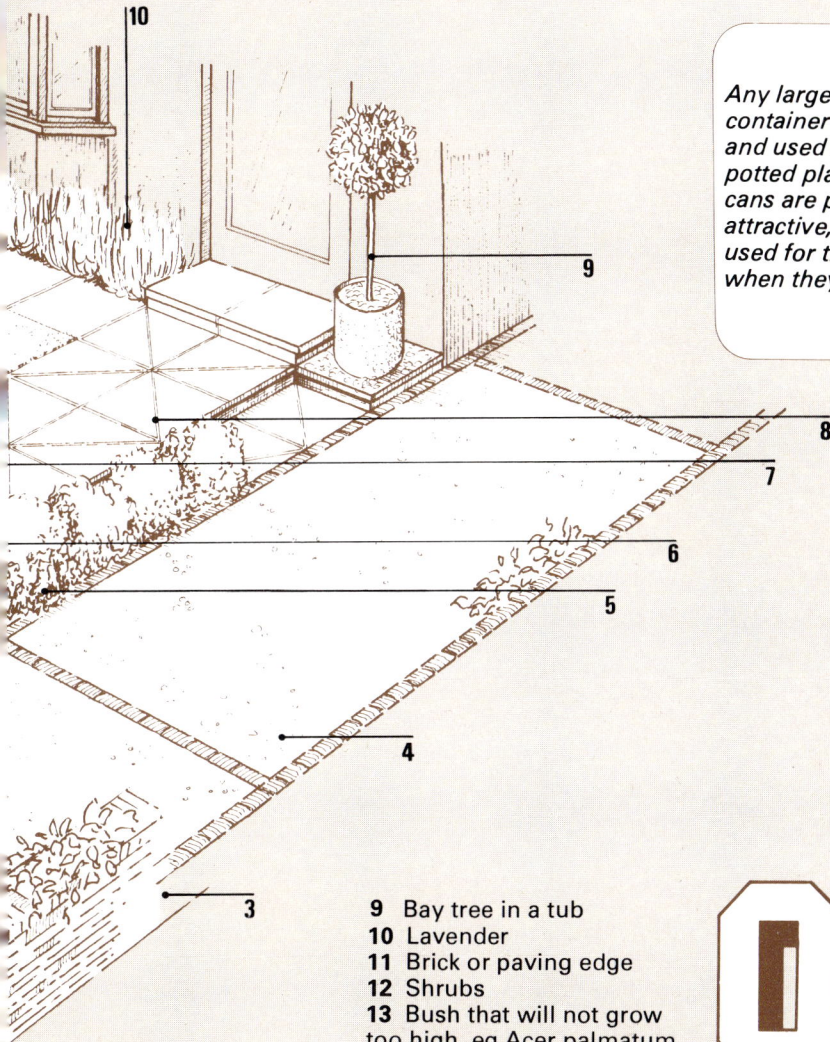

10

9

8

7

6

5

4

3

Any large metal container can be painted and used for holding potted plants. Watering cans are particularly attractive, and can be used for this purpose when they spring a leak.

9 Bay tree in a tub
10 Lavender
11 Brick or paving edge
12 Shrubs
13 Bush that will not grow too high, eg Acer palmatum, Rhus typhina 'Laciniata' or Amelanchier laevis

05

There will not be much scope for radically altering the basic shape of a front garden, especially in a suburban area, where the format often includes a drive on one side and a wall or fence separating the house from its neighbours. These man-made factors can be softened by the clever use of plants. It is also important to ensure that paths and drives are planned and constructed carefully for safety.

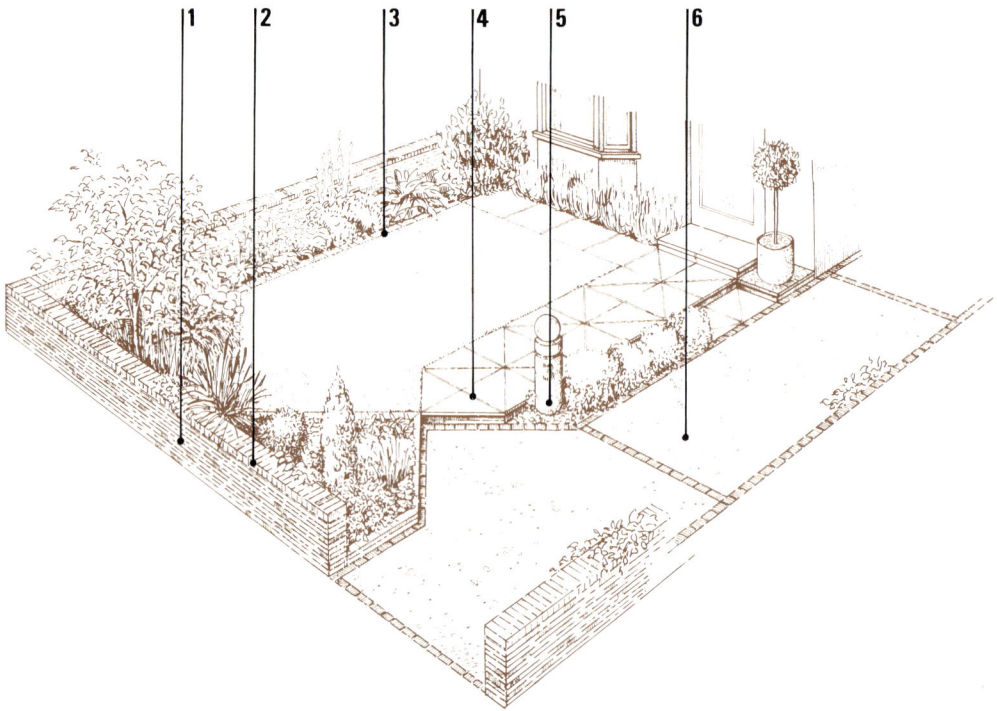

1
Walls in brick or setts to match house.
2
Low walls give a good view to the car emerging from the drive.
3
Lawn edge of brick or paving to act as mowing strip.

4
Path (pages 92–5) veers left to direct pedestrians, and is made of triangular paving stone in 'non-slip' texture in single colour to match the drive. Shape allows for a change in direction without the need for odd stones which could work loose and lift.

5
Base of bollard in concrete to match drive. Light illuminates path and step.
6
Drive formed into panels by granite setts or hard bricks, filled with exposed concrete or tarmac. It should be left uncluttered as it is narrow.

The main function of plants in a front garden is usually to soften the hard lines of paths, walls and drives. They can also be valuable in disguising inspection covers, drains and inlets. It is best to plant shrubs, trees and flowers which are simple and easy to care for. It is useful to bear in mind that they are there to complement the house, not to detract from or obscure it.

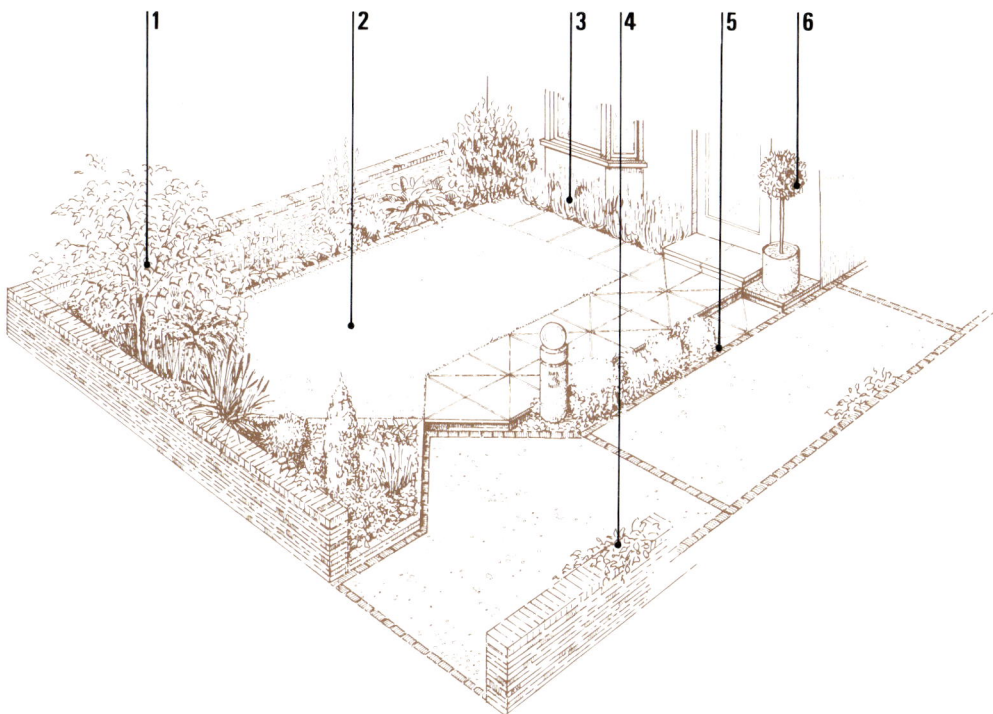

1
Corner bush gives height and provides a focal point.
2
Main area left as lawn (pages 80–3) to give a feeling of peace.
3
Lavender can hide air vents.

4
Climbing plants soften a severe wall (page 73).
5
Low plants allow easy opening of car door.
6
Bay tree gives an air of importance to the front entrance.

A suburban back garden

Rapid growth of suburban development and migration to the perimeters of towns has resulted in a broad similarity of suburban plots in both form and general layout. Size will vary, but the essential feature of this type of back garden will be a uniformity of terrain and a regular shape. There is no need to make extravagant changes: a good design can produce a garden with individuality at reasonable cost, within a defined surrounding.

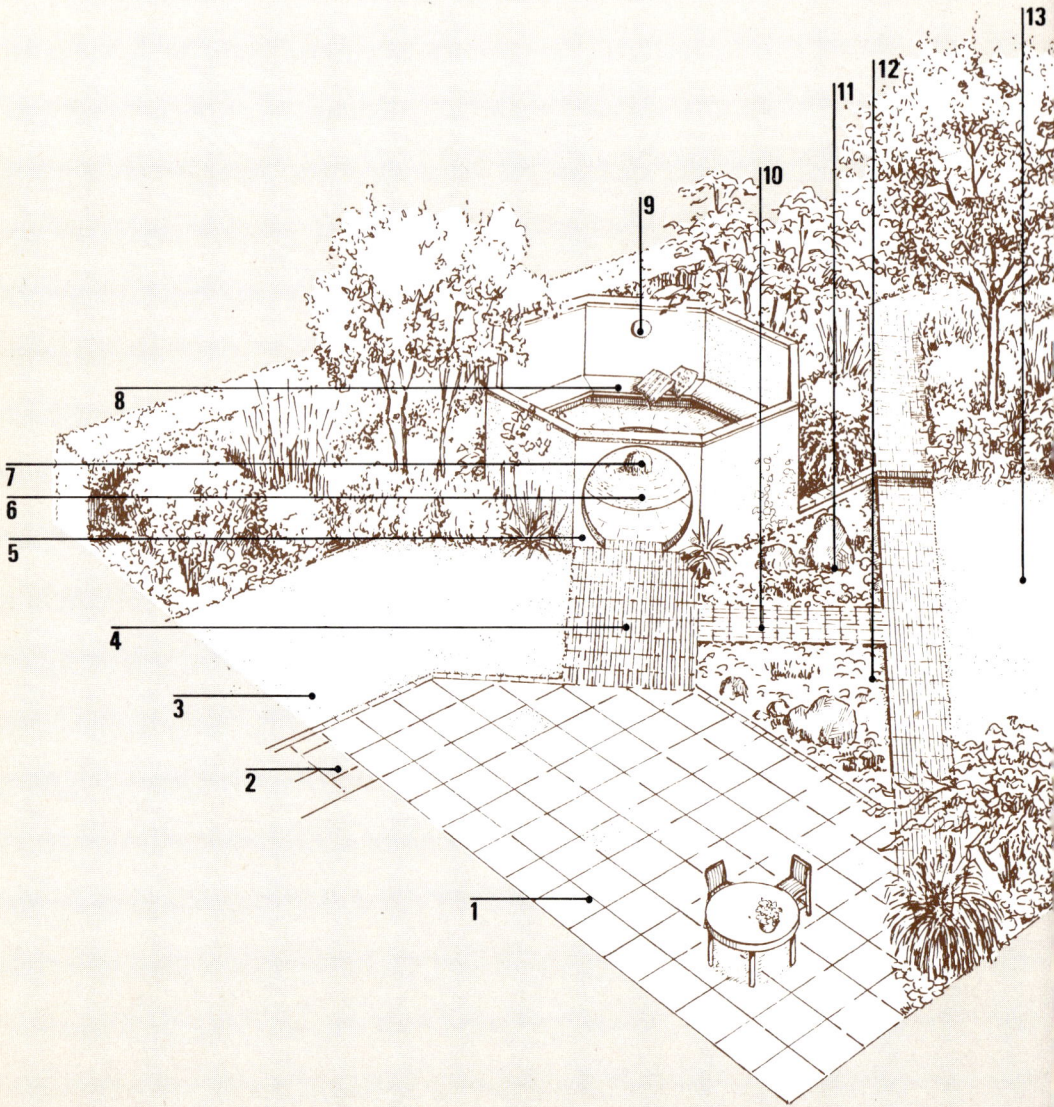

The labelled garden illustration shows numbered callouts 15, 16, 17, 18, 19, 20, 21, 22, 23, 24, 25, 26 pointing to features in the garden scene.

Many people find a border of silver-leaved plants pleasant. These include:

Lavatera
Leontopodium
(Edelweiss)
Nepeta (Catmint)
Ruta graveolens (Rue)
Senecio greyi
Stachys lanata

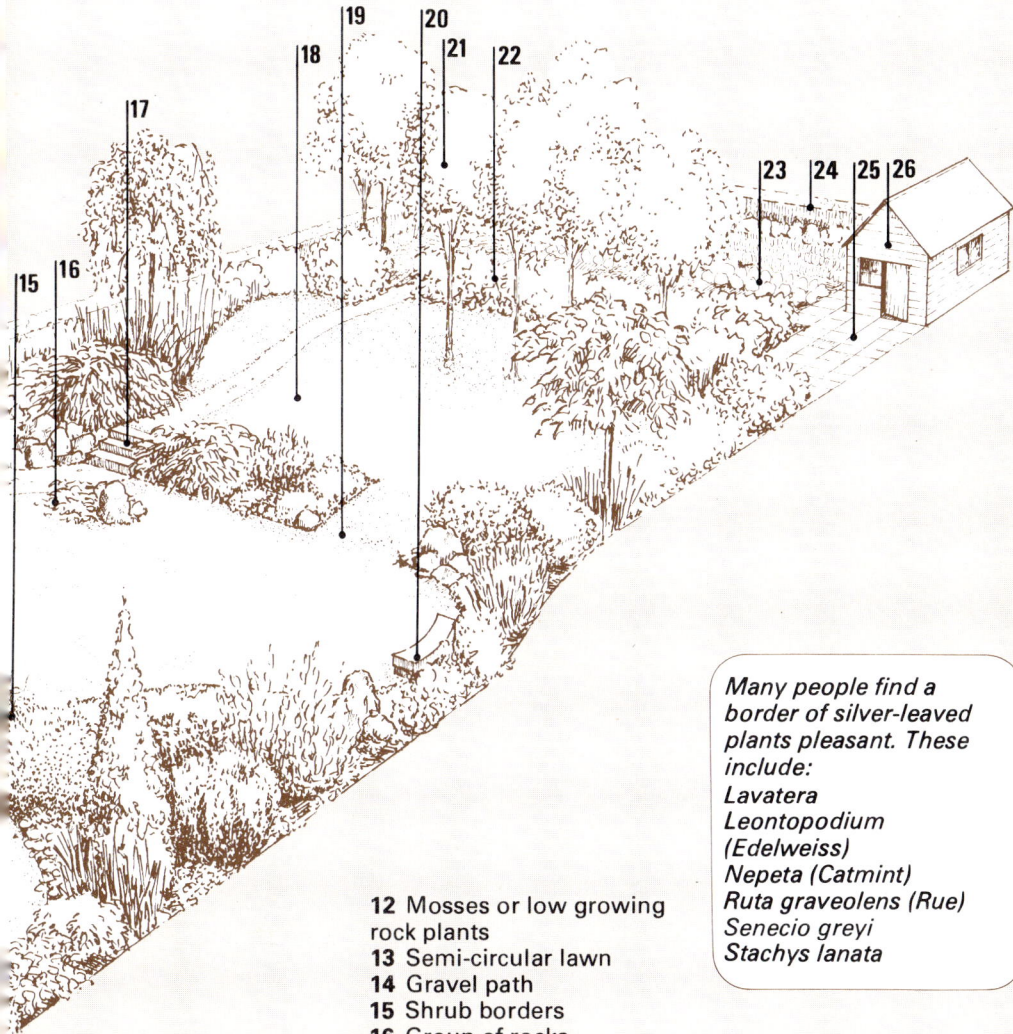

1 Large patio
2 Path to front of house
3 Lawn
4 Brick path
5 Enclosed octagonal area
6 Circular ornamental pool
7 Bubble fountain
8 Seat
9 Wall light
10 Narrower brick path
11 Boulders and pebbles
12 Mosses or low growing rock plants
13 Semi-circular lawn
14 Gravel path
15 Shrub borders
16 Group of rocks
17 Steps
18 Upper lawn
19 Embankment
20 Simple stone bench
21 Group of light trees
22 Informal evergreen hedge
23 Vegetable garden
24 Boundary hedge or fence
25 Utility area
26 Good-sized shed

06

Plan of projected gardens in
village at Ilford in 1848.

1
Trees (page 86)
surrounding enclosed area
put walls into scale, and
integrate the area into the
garden.
2
Secluded sitting area
(page 59), illuminated at
night to provide a focal
point.

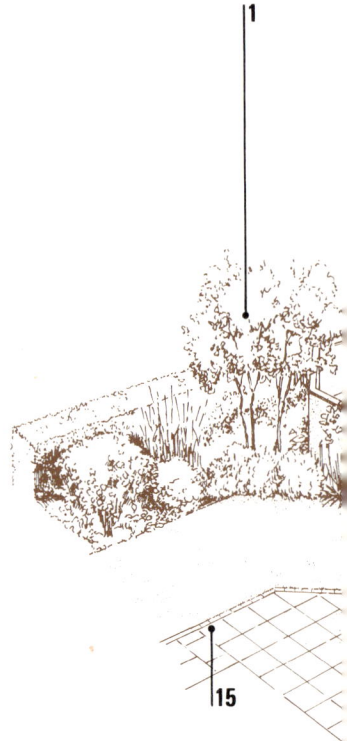

9
Changes in ground level
can be artificially
introduced to provide
interest in an otherwise flat
area.
10
Gentle grassed slope
facilitates mowing.

3
Path deliberately bends out of view.
4
Gravel path gives air of informality and softness.
5
Path through grass gives false sense of width.

6
Hedge (page 84) to screen vegetable garden.
7
Longer grass in upper lawn, which can be used as children's play area.

8
Trees screen view of house next door, and have been brought forward from the far boundary to make room for the vegetable garden. Bulbs can be planted underneath.

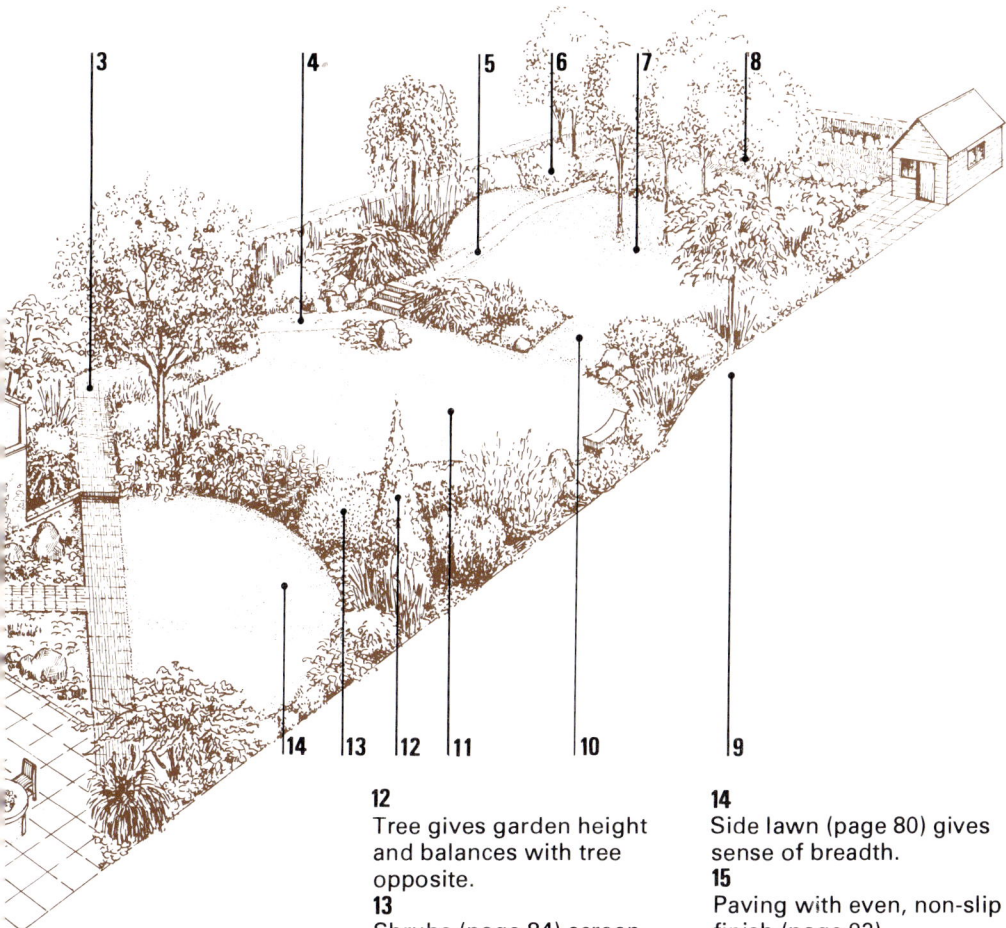

12
Tree gives garden height and balances with tree opposite.
13
Shrubs (page 84) screen second area and provide interest.

14
Side lawn (page 80) gives sense of breadth.
15
Paving with even, non-slip finish (page 92).

11
Lawn terminates first general area, which is formal in character.

A roof garden

As long ago as 600 BC, there were roof gardens on elevated terraces in Babylon. These became known as the 'Hanging Gardens' and were one of the Seven Wonders of the World. Archaeological evidence suggests that these gardens may have been planted on temple arches 75 ft (23 m) high, and watered by a complex system of irrigation from nearby rivers.

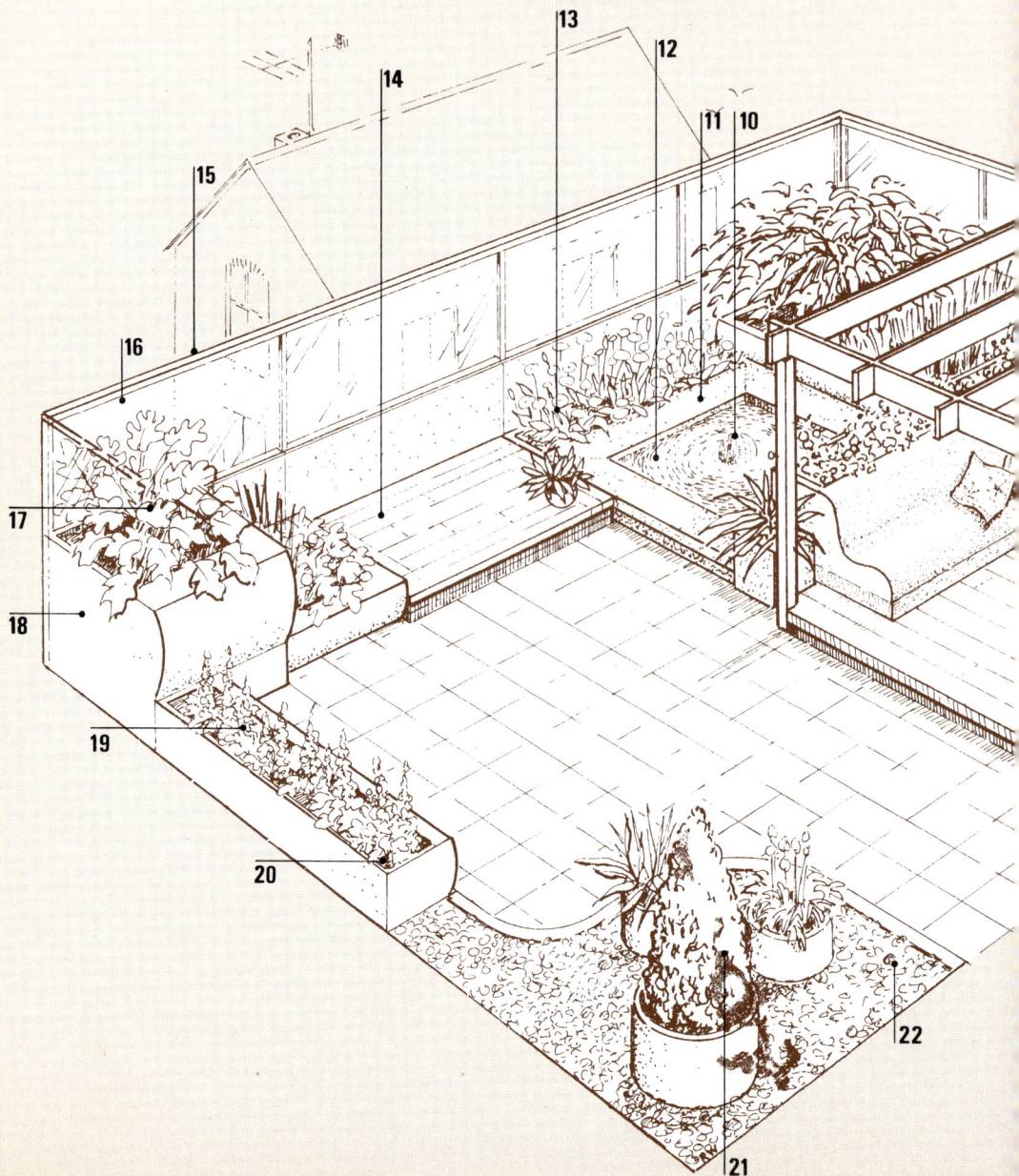

Modern methods and materials mean that roof gardens today do not require such miraculous feats of engineering, but there are still several technical considerations to be taken into account. In the initial stages, an architect or surveyor should be consulted to establish the load-bearing properties of the flat roof. Materials should be light, and the weight of the garden users considered. Other location problems concern exposure. Wind (page 72) will damage plants if there are tall buildings nearby producing air currents. It is usually necessary to construct a strong transparent barrier for protection and safety. There will be need for a drainage system. These details impose some restrictions on the design, but roof gardens can give the atmosphere of a cultivated area with only a few well-selected plants in attractive tubs, providing a private area for entertaining, sunbathing and enjoying the open air.

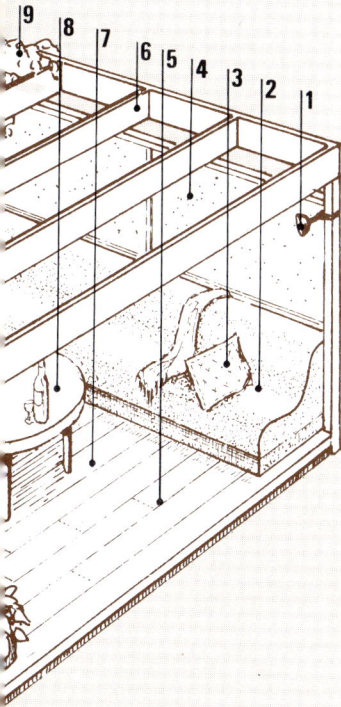

1 Spotlight
2 Fibreglass units
3 Scatter cushions
4 Textured opaque panels
5 Red cedar deckwork
6 Overhead struts of timber or plastic
7 Sitting area
8 Low table
9 Light climbers
10 Bubble fountain
11 Textured fibreglass
12 Small pool
13 Annual bedding
14 Raised red cedar deck
15 Anodized aluminium alloy frames
16 Transparent smoked or tinted glass over fibreglass or aluminium solid panels
17 Hardy shrubs
18 Fibreglass planters
19 Annual bedding
20 Lightweight compost
21 Dwarf conifer in pot
22 Lightweight aggregate
23 Lightweight tiles stuck with bitumen compound

07

1
Panels prevent view over other gardens and act as a screen.
2
Raised deck for viewing.
3
Glass surround protects plants without spoiling the view.

4
Pool (pages 120–5) needs only enough water to accommodate small circulating submersible pump. If interior is painted black, reflection is heightened.

5
Bubble fountain provides sound of water without loss of water, which is usual in a tall fountain.
6
Overhead struts provide screening when viewed at an angle from windows higher up.
7
Hollow fibreglass seating units are light, strong and easy to clean.
8
Cushions add colour.
9
Roof may need reinforcing.
10
Paving slopes to aggregate.
11
Aggregate provides interesting texture, covers surface water drainage system, and is a foil for plant pots.
12
Fibreglass containers and lightweight compost help with the weight problem. These composts need a regular feeding programme as they are not very nutrient retentive. Watering systems can be installed in containers.
13
Tall shrubs (page 84) give height and frame the view.
14
Plants should be tolerant to wind (page 72). None appears above the surround.
15
Windows could extend along this side.

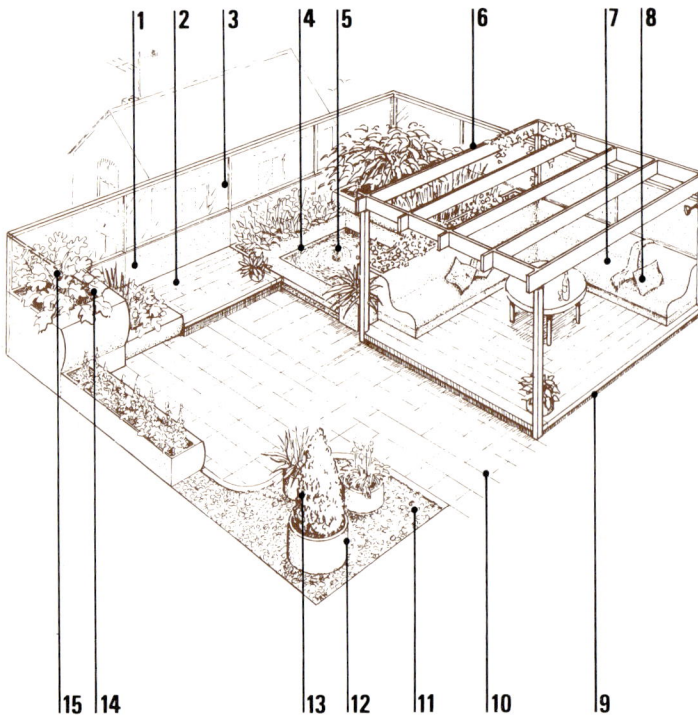

Patios

A patio is a paved area where people can sit outdoors in the sunshine when weather permits. Usually a patio is between house and garden, but if the house faces north it may be sited elsewhere. If it is roofed over, too, it may make the house rooms rather dark. In a small city garden, the whole garden area may be used as a patio, and this can be extremely attractive. A patio can also be made on a flat roof when space is limited. But wherever it is built, the patio is likely to present the same problems and to require very similar solutions.

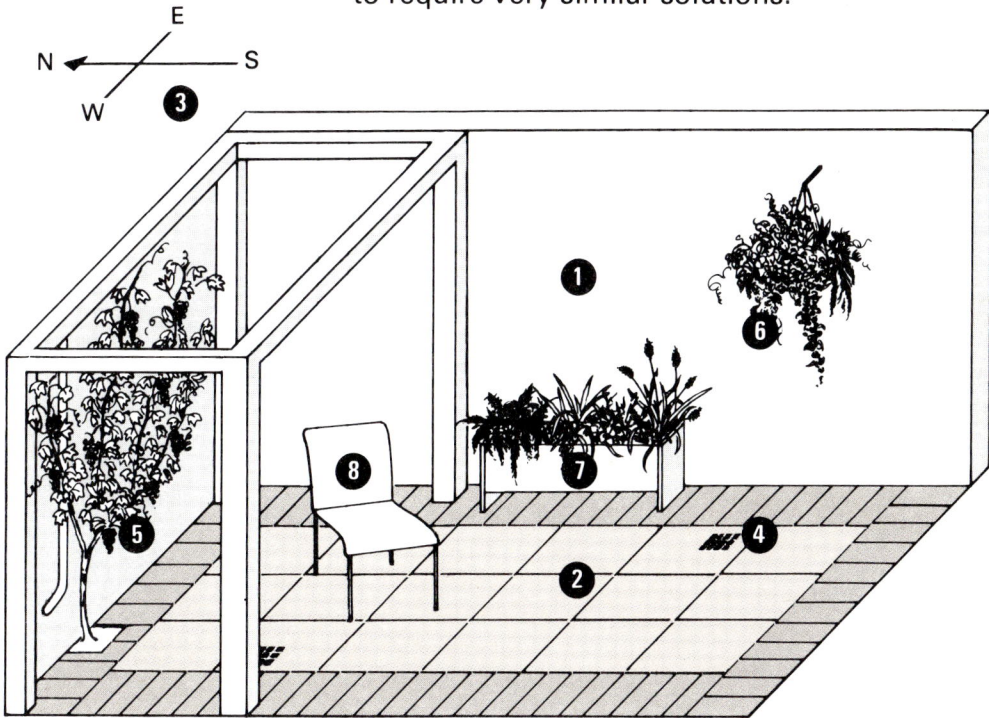

1 Walls around a patio are best finished in a light colour.

2 Floors may be of stone, wood, brick, concrete, tiles etc, but must be level so that chairs do not rock.

3 The patio should face south if possible, and be sheltered on north and east.

4 Adequate drainage is essential.

5 Climbing plants hide many an eyesore.

6 Containers fixed to the wall, or baskets hanging from the roof, may be filled with bright blooms, and make up for a lack of tall trees by varying the height.

7 Tubs and troughs also give a glow of colour, attracting the attention.

8 Since patios are intended for relaxation, seating is especially important. Chairs may be left there or taken indoors in bad weather (if you have any storage space for them). If your patio is on a roof, you also need space to store tools there, and some way to dispose of the inevitable rubbish.

An overlooked garden

Many difficulties which present themselves to the garden planner arise on the site itself or are the result of special requirements on the part of the garden user. Here the major problem is an external feature – a tall block of flats beyond the furthest corner of the garden which overlooks the site. This design could be applied to any similar problem of location, and has been developed to show how it is possible to screen unwelcome sights without turning the garden into a prison yard, retaining a natural aspect.

To encourage butterflies you should plant Sedum spectabile (Ice plant), michaelmas daisies or buddleia. But you will also get caterpillars! Still, caterpillars will also bring some more birds to your garden.

1 Lawn
2 Patio of rectangular paving
3 Utility/drying area of rectangular paving
4 Formal pool and fountain
5 L-shaped sunken lawn
6 Screened utility area
7 Weeping tree
8 Dense trees to screen an eyesore, such as Populus alba, Acer platanoides or Prunus avium, will give privacy to sitting area
9 Main sitting area
10 Open slatted cedar or white painted structure
11 Cedar deckwork supported off ground
12 Mowing strips
13 Path
14 Seat
15 High boundary wall

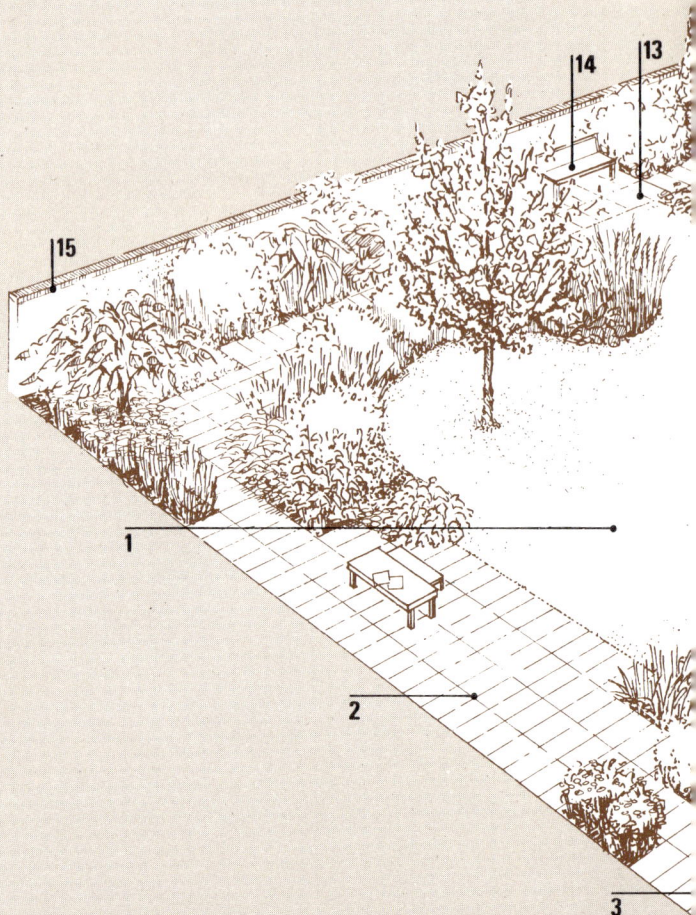

If you are fond of a stroll in the garden in the evening, plant clumps of scented flowers here and there, eg tobacco plants or night-scented stock. You can then go on enjoying flowers even when it is too dark to see them.

11

10

9

8

7

6

12

5

4

08

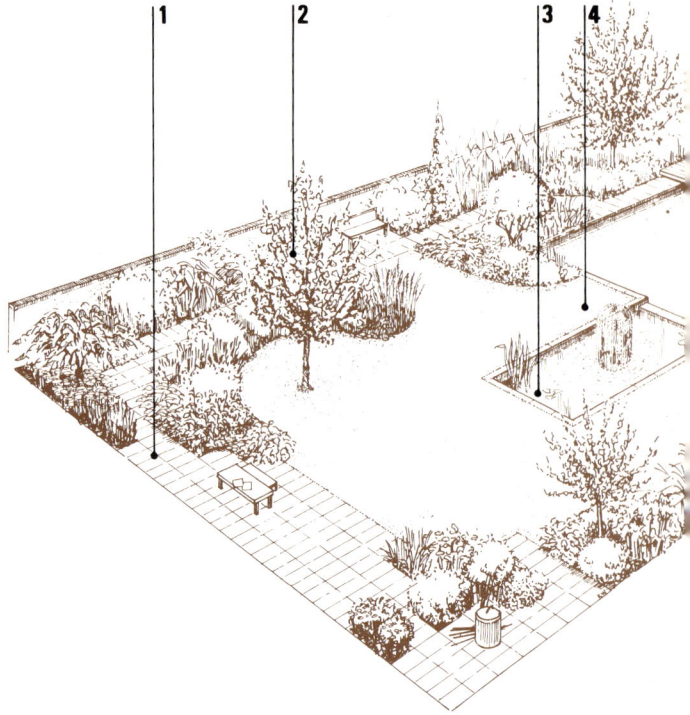

In addition to the problem of an overlooked garden, considered above, there may be many other serious difficulties for the gardener to overcome.

1   Natural problems: wind (page 72), exposure, growing conditions, animal pests (page 46).

2   Age: if new, may need fast-growing plants in the beginning; if old, may need to change existing features.

3   Shape: either too regular, or difficult — triangular, narrow, wide, small, large.

4   Location: near traffic, high rise development, suburban plot near others, corner plot.

Elaborate Italian cascade on steep sloping problem site.

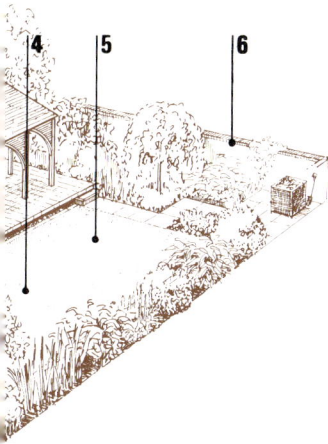

1
Slabs laid to give sense of direction.

2
Tree (pages 86–7) is centre of the circular area of lawn and provides some screening.

3
Pool (pages 120–5) forms a central focal point. The garden has no outward views, so this feature provides interest from both ends of the garden.

4
Usual arrangement of formal area near house and informal area away from it has been reversed as it is likely that the garden will be viewed in summer looking towards house.

5
Formal L-shaped lawn (pages 80–3) is more in keeping with sitting area.

6
Height of wall (pages 108–9) and distance of path away from it are important considerations for making screening more effective.

Other aspects of the problem could be:
Design: given existing restrictions and needs, how to make the most attractive solution.
Cost: of maintenance or of new design.

Difficult features: organic – soil problems (pages 22–3 and 26–27); natural – drainage (pages 24–5), trees in wrong place, rocks on site; man-made – paths (pages 92–5), built-up areas in bad repair or wrong position.

Requirements: recreation, children's play areas (page 117), vegetable growing (pages 138–9), privacy, entertaining, utility areas (pages 118–9).
Maintenance: easy care for elderly, invalid or busy families (pages 134–7); how to make hard work most productive.

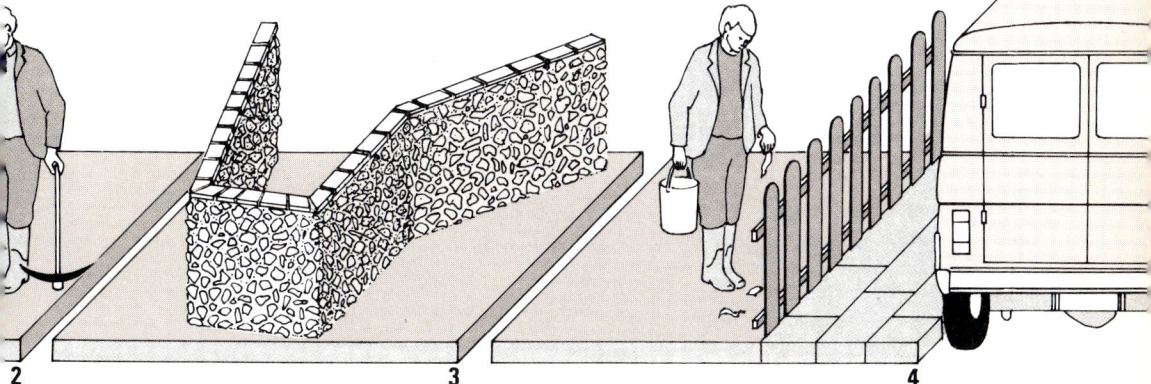

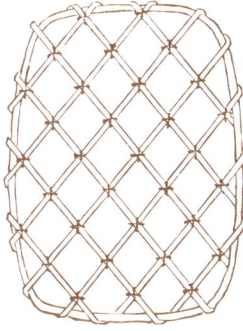

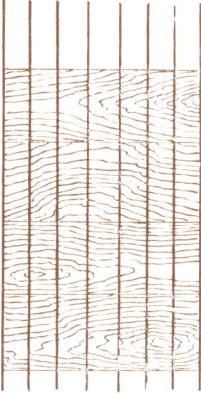

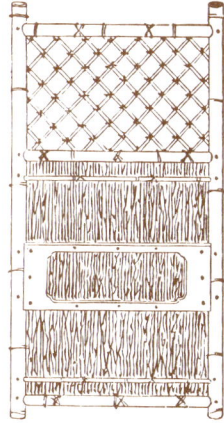
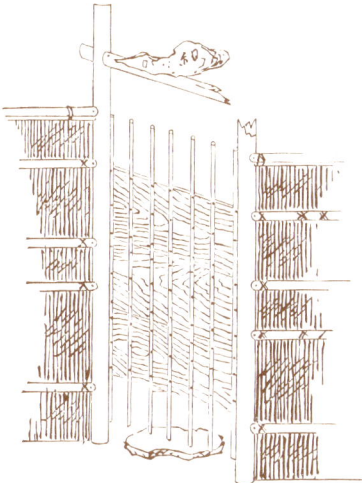
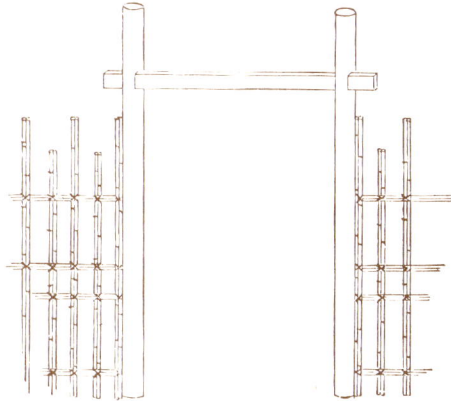

Chapter three
Special features

Most gardens contain a mixture of things: a few beds of flowers, a shrub or two, perhaps a tree, some paths, with steps if the site is uneven, a fence or wall around the boundary, a garden seat, a short hedge.

Depending on the taste of the gardener, the proportions of these ingredients can vary considerably: a really keen gardener may devote almost the entire area to annual bedding plants or vegetables; a man who is more keen on building than on digging may construct lots of paths, concrete steps and walls, thus reducing the amount of soil surface he has to tend; and an elderly couple may well decide to have several garden seats, sheltered by walls, where they and their friends can rest during a tour of the garden to enjoy the view.

But such extremes are not often found, although four such gardens are illustrated here. Most people will take an idea or two from each of them, and create their own individual combination of features.

Spring is a busy time of year, with upkeep and new projects.

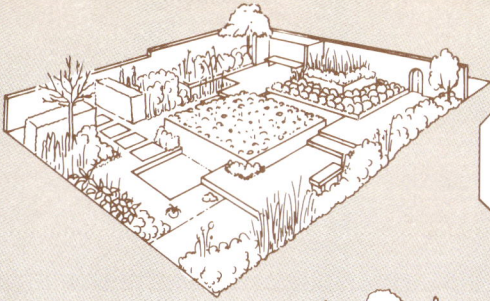

09 The energetic gardener who enjoys raising annuals and planting them out can plan for a riot of colour.

10 Lawns, trees and shrubs are predominantly green, but this makes for a soothing and refreshing garden.

11 Large areas of paving, with variations in colour and texture, are both easy to maintain and good-looking.

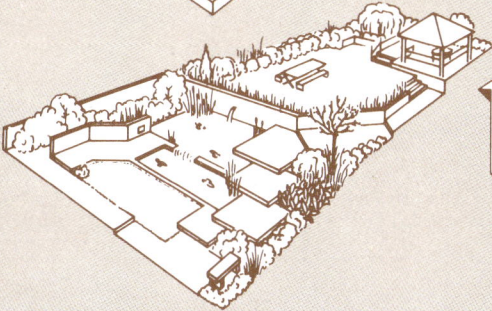

12 Paths and steps are necessary in most gardens, but a steep site can make them a striking feature of the landscape.

13 Fences, walls, screens and garden furniture can be useful and ornamental if they are carefully chosen and sited.

A flower garden

This is a garden for the flower-grower, with just a few trees and hedges to give variation in height. The garden is on a slight slope, and the lower area around the pool is suitable for damp-loving plants. Shade-loving flowers such as foxgloves flourish under the trees. And in the open raised beds grow all the sun-loving flowers, at a convenient height for planting, and well-drained. Tall plants such as hollyhocks, red hot pokers, thistles and lupins are in the side beds, and a few climbers over the pergola.

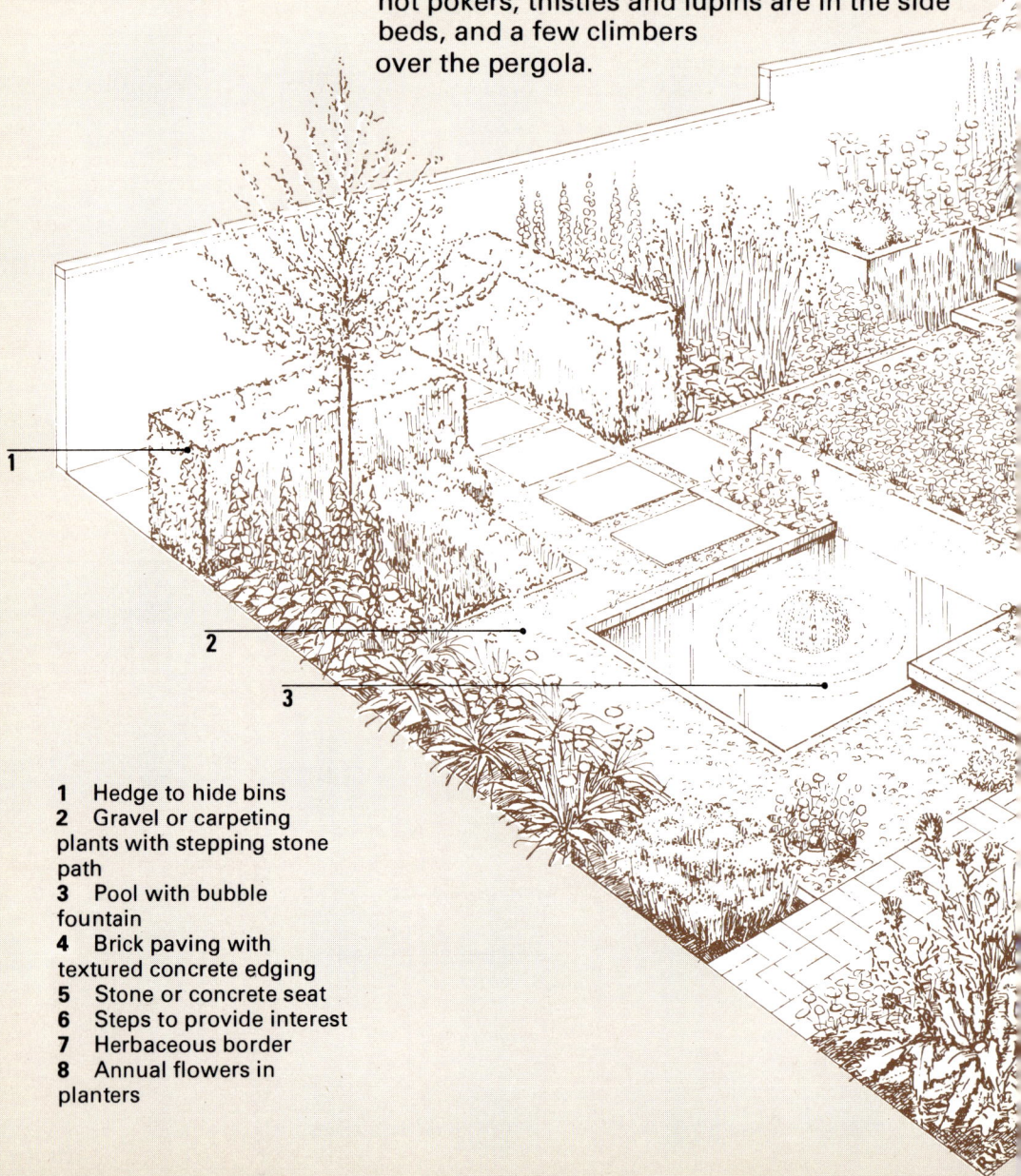

1 Hedge to hide bins
2 Gravel or carpeting plants with stepping stone path
3 Pool with bubble fountain
4 Brick paving with textured concrete edging
5 Stone or concrete seat
6 Steps to provide interest
7 Herbaceous border
8 Annual flowers in planters

If you are growing flowers to be picked for the house, remove side buds: then all the plant's energy will go into producing the main bloom.

Plan each flower bed so that there will always be something interesting to see. Many gardeners like to include a number of plants with striking foliage among their flowers, because the ornamental leaves will continue to provide an attractive display when the flowers are over. Bear in mind the flowering time, the height and the colour of each species when you plan, and try to place them tastefully. Put low plants near the paths, and keep tall ones for the back of side beds or the middle of central ones.

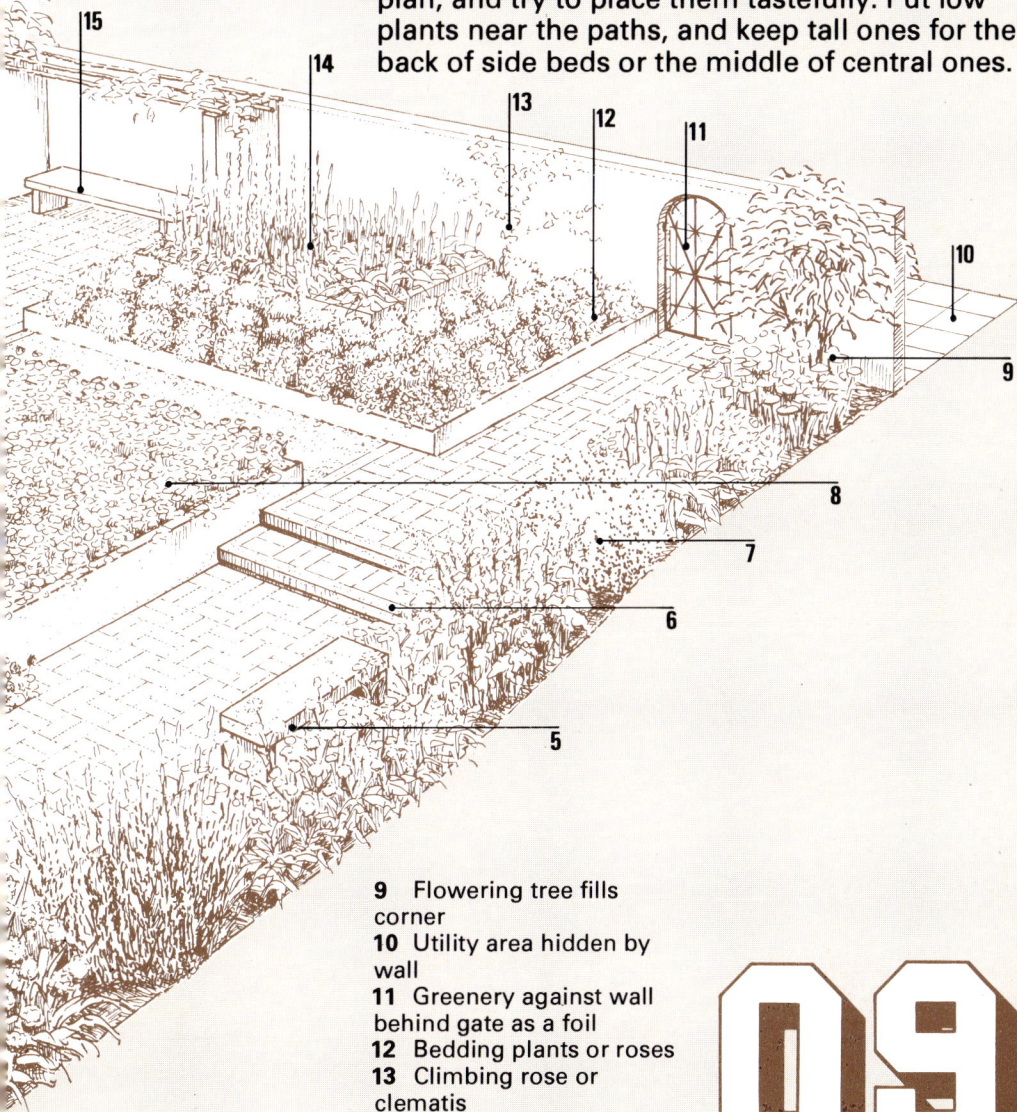

9 Flowering tree fills corner
10 Utility area hidden by wall
11 Greenery against wall behind gate as a foil
12 Bedding plants or roses
13 Climbing rose or clematis
14 Tall flowers give height
15 Seat under climbing rose or wistaria

09

Plants

Most gardens contain plants of many different kinds: small and larger plants, shrubs and usually a tree or two. Some of these plants appear almost unaffected by the coldest winter weather, whereas some die at the first touch of frost. Annuals live for only a short time, but provide a wonderful burst of colour during the summer months; evergreen shrubs live for many years, always looking the same. When choosing plants, take their growing habits into account. In particular, do find out how tall and how wide they will become, before it's too late!

Most flowers and vegetables are **herbaceous** plants: they have non-woody stems and they usually die down in the winter. Many herbaceous plants are **annuals**, which live for only one season. **Hardy annuals** are planted as seeds outdoors, often in the autumn, and survive frosts and bad weather.

Half-hardy annuals dislike cold, so they are planted indoors or in a frame, and planted out when the frosts are over. **Greenhouse annuals** have to be grown indoors all the time. **Biennials** live for two years: planted in spring or early summer, they produce only leaves the first year, then rest through the winter, and bloom in the second year, before dying. **Perennials** live for several years, once they are established: stems and leaves die back in winter, but roots remain alive, and the plants grow new shoots and leaves each spring.

When you have to move plants, choose your day carefully. The garden soil should be damp but not too wet. The plants should have been hardened off if grown in a greenhouse or frame, by gradually introducing them to colder weather: leaving windows open, or moving the seed boxes or pots outdoors for increasing intervals. If you are planting perennials, the bed should be treated with compost or manure first, because the plants will be there for several years; annuals are less demanding because they will be there for only a few months, and they will often flower better in poor soil.

When tying a plant to a stake, wrap string around the plant loosely and then cross it before wrapping it around the stake and tying a knot. The string is then less likely to cut into the stem and gives more play.

Bulbs, corms and tubers are special forms of perennials, some hardy and others in need of careful attention. Some kinds of bulbs have to be lifted after flowering, and stored indoors until the next season. But many other bulbs can be left in the ground from year to year, unless they become over-crowded.

Woody plants are perennials that have strong woody stems (or trunks). **Deciduous trees** and shrubs are woody plants that lose their leaves in autumn and grow new ones in spring. **Evergreen trees** and shrubs keep their leaves throughout the year. **Conifers** grow their seeds in cones, and their evergreen leaves are needle-shaped. Evergreens do occasionally replace their leaves, but the leaves fall off a few at a time throughout the year, so that the tree is never completely bare. **Semi-evergreens** retain their leaves throughout a mild winter, but lose them in a severe one.

Dig a large hole, deep enough to allow the soil mark on the tree to be just *below* the ground surface; the hole should be wide enough to let the roots spread out. Soil removed from the hole is mixed with compost or leaf mould. Drive in a stake if this will be needed. Make a small mound in the middle of the hole, and spread the roots over it, so that they slope downwards. Keep the tree upright, and spread the soil over the roots, firming down as you go along. If trees are bought in a hessian container, they can be planted in it, but it is better removed. When the tree is in place, give it a good watering, and attach it to the supporting stake.

The plants you choose for your garden will be dictated partly by the kind of soil you have. Your neighbours' gardens will also give you a hint on what is likely to do well in your own. Spend some time in the shop, reading seed packets, which will tell you what conditions the plants need. Your local library will have books specializing in various kinds of plants, eg roses or dahlias, which will go into more detail than any general gardening book can. And most gardeners like being asked for their advice.

Some areas of your garden, if not the whole of it, may have special problems. One part of it may be in deep shade, and here you must choose plants that actually prefer shade, if you are to get a good display; if you do manage to grow ordinary plants there, they will never do as well as they should. Sometimes there is a long narrow passageway between two houses, which is not only shady but also windy, because the wind is channelled through the narrow gap. And town gardens have special problems, such as poor soil and polluted air, and are often shaded for most of the day by tall buildings.

Besides the soil, you have also to bear in mind the use of certain parts of the garden. Don't plant rose bushes near the clothes line, or where they will overhang a narrow path. And in a border, you must put tall plants at the back and low ones at the front. Group flowers by the colour type: bright shades tend to overpower delicate ones.

Ten plants that grow well in shade
Anemone
Aquilegia
Astilbe
Convallaria (lily of the valley)
Hosta
Lobelia
Polygonum
Primula
Saxifraga (mossy types)
Many ferns

Ten plants that grow well in windy areas
Alyssum
Anemone
Centaurea (cornflower)
Geranium
Kentranthus (Valerian)
Malva
Potentilla
Scabious
Sedum
Stachys

Ten plants that grow well in dry situations
Achillea
Alyssum
Geranium
Iris
Kniphofia
Lupin
Lychnis
Nepeta (Catmint)
Sedum
Veronica

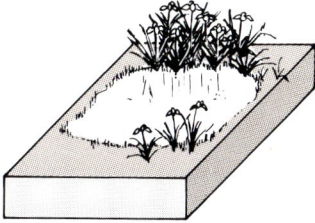

Ten plants that grow well in moist areas
Astilbe
Hosta
Iris
Lobelia cardinalis
Mimulus (musk)
Phlox
Primula
Pulmonaria
Ranunculus
Trollius

Ten plants that grow well in clay soil
Aster
Astilbe
Caltha
Campanula
Geranium
Hosta
Iris
Polygonum
Primula
Salvia

Ten plants that grow well in chalk and limestone
Alyssum
Centaurea (cornflower)
Clematis
Dianthus (pink)
Gypsophila
Hypericum
Lathyrus (sweet pea)
Linaria
Peony
Scabious

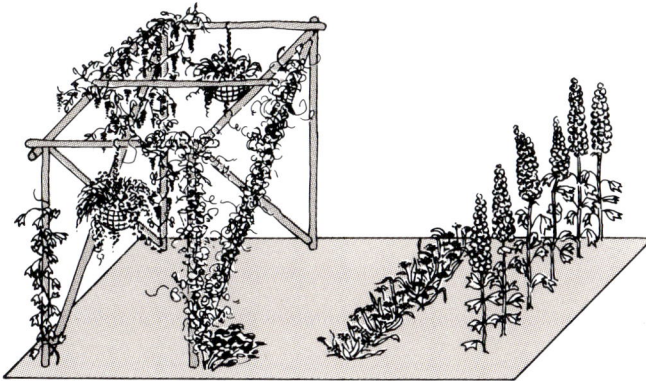

Hardy climbing plants
Clematis
Hedera (ivy)
Humulus (hop)
Lonicera (honeysuckle)
Virginia creepers

Plants for hanging baskets
Campanula isophyllum
Fuchsia
Pelargonium peltatum
(ivy-leaved geranium)
Tradescantia
Tropaeolum (nasturtium)

Five low flowers
Ageratum
Helleborus
Lobelia
Mesembryanthemum
Viola

Five tall flowers
Delphinium
Gladiolus
Lily
Lupin
Helianthus

Above: The soil of your garden will probably favour some kinds of plants and handicap others. If your soil contains much lime, you will not succeed in growing rhododendrons, although other shrubs such as berberis and buddleia should do well. It is better to do some careful planning, and choose plants that *will* succeed.

Sometimes a dull corner or a patio can be brightened by a windowbox, tub or hanging basket. Remember that they will need good soil and frequent watering in dry weather, as they are too shallow to retain moisture. A wall can often be improved by a climbing plant, either on the wall or on a trellis.

No gardening plan can apply everywhere. In the north, the growing season may be 2 or 3 weeks later, and a cold spell delays plants too.

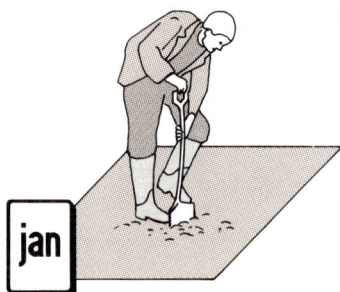

jan

January
Plan your garden, and order seed. Dig areas for early planting if weather permits. Cover hydrangeas with straw to protect them from the frost. Plant lilies and begonias indoors. Prune climbing roses.

feb

February
Prune or plant roses. Prune summer jasmine and some clematis. Sow seed for bedding plants, in house, greenhouse or warm frame. Repot house plants if they need it, and plant indoor bulbs outside when they finish flowering.

mar

March
Plant autumn-sown sweet peas outdoors, also hardy perennials (delphiniums, lupins, phlox). Plant summer bulbs (gladioli, montbretia). Transplant hellebores and irises if necessary. Spray roses. Plant forsythia and weigela. Sow half-hardy annuals indoors.

jul

July
Spray against mildew and greenfly. Lift and store daffodils, tulips and hyacinths. Take cuttings of helianthemums and pinks, and from shrubs. Remove all the side buds from chrysanthemums.

aug

August
Plant bulbs indoors for Christmas, also freesias for January flowering. Plant autumn crocuses, hardy cyclamen and Madonna lilies outdoors. Sow hardy annuals for next year. Take pelargonium and calceolaria cuttings. Cut evergreen hedges.

sep

September
Plant bulbs outdoors for next spring, also hardy lilies. Plant bulbs in pots for winter. Plant shrubs and evergreens. Sow hardy annuals. Bring bedding plants inside for winter, and chrysanthemums for indoor flowering. Take cuttings of pelargoniums and other bedding plants. Start new compost heap.

April
Move spring bulbs to secluded bed when flowering ends. Sow hardy annuals outside, also grass seed. Plant conifers and evergreens. Plant out early chrysanthemums. Put fertilizer on roses. Prune forsythia and flowering currant after flowering.

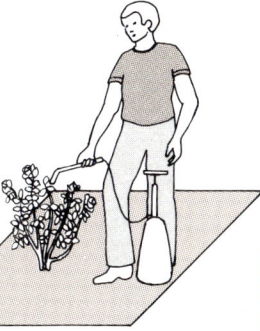

May
Divide and move spring-flowering perennials. Plant out half-hardy annuals (zinnias, antirrhinums) and dahlias. Pinch tops out of early chrysanthemums. Stake herbaceous plants. Spray roses against aphids. Mulch shrubs. Sow wallflowers and other biennials.

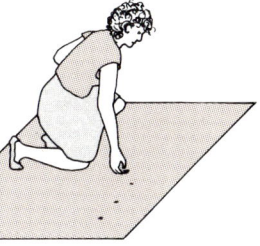

June
Sow sweet williams and lupins outdoors, and indoor primulas and cinerarias. Put half-hardy plants outside. Divide May-flowering perennials if necessary. Prune weigela, spiraea and lilac after flowering. Spray roses against aphids.

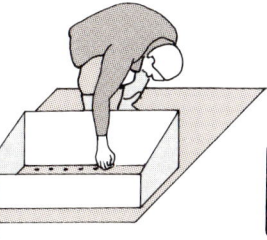

October
Lift dahlias, montbretia and gladioli after first frost, dry and store in cellar. Lift summer bedding plants, and store perennials in cold frame or greenhouse. Prepare soil for planting polyanthus and wallflowers. Plant roses and deciduous trees. Sow sweet peas in cold frame, and plant biennials and perennials.

November
Plant outdoor tulip bulbs, also hardy perennials. Put chrysanthemums into cold frame for winter. Prune any deciduous hedges. Tidy beds and rockery. Add lime if necessary.

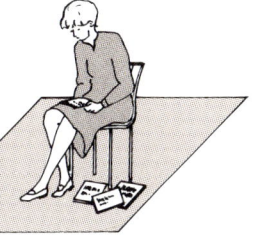

December
Protect outdoor plants against slugs. Winter pruning. Keep an eye on stored tubers. Plan for next year.

A green garden

This is a garden for the person who prefers grass, shrubs and trees to the usual gaudy flower beds. The lawn takes up a large part of the area, and will need a good deal of mowing in summer. On the other hand, many shrubs and trees require little attention except for pruning, which is usually done during the winter months. Trees and shrubs are expensive, compared with a packet of seeds, but a varied collection can be built up gradually over the years, and you can take cuttings from them later.

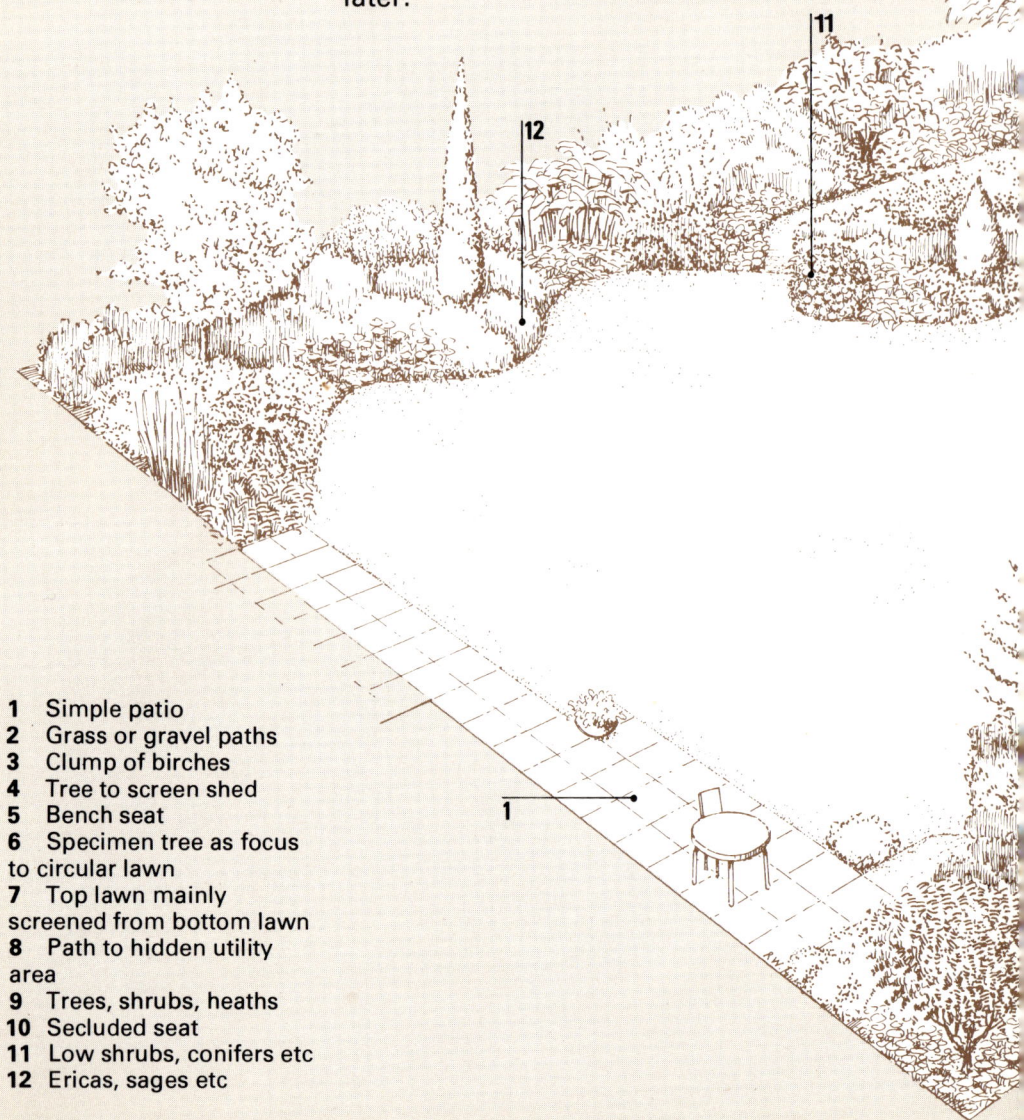

1 Simple patio
2 Grass or gravel paths
3 Clump of birches
4 Tree to screen shed
5 Bench seat
6 Specimen tree as focus to circular lawn
7 Top lawn mainly screened from bottom lawn
8 Path to hidden utility area
9 Trees, shrubs, heaths
10 Secluded seat
11 Low shrubs, conifers etc
12 Ericas, sages etc

6

5

7

8

9

4

3

2

Ferns are very useful to fill in a shady corner, especially:
Asplenium scolopendrium (Hart's tongue)
Dryopteris cristata (Crested buckler fern)
Matteuccia struthiopteris (Ostrich-feather fern)
Polystichum aculeatum (Hard shield fern)

10

Much of the charm of this garden comes from the restfulness of its varied shades of green. Almost all leaves are green, but there their similarity ends. The colour of the shrubs varies from the pale yellowish green of Japanese maple to the sombre shade of evergreens such as laurel and yew. Leaves may be shiny and smooth, or rather woolly and soft; some are narrow and spiky, whereas others are broad and flat. The shape of the whole plant varies too, from the vertical spire to the horizontal ground-cover.

1
Like other plants, conifers too have varying tastes about where to grow. Most of them like plenty of light, but some species will grow happily in shady places. Pfitzer's juniper makes a splendid ground-cover even in dense shade, and one of the golden yews will lighten a dark corner attractively.

2
Lawns require a good deal of maintenance (see pages 80–3). Apart from the regular mowing during the summer, they also need to be treated with weedkillers to deal with the daisies and moss; and if overhanging trees make them very damp, they must be spiked to improve the drainage. The grass also needs fertilizer.

3
One excellent way to save work is to plant around the edges of your lawn with various prostrate shrubs, preferably evergreens. Many kinds of juniper, cotoneaster and heath are suitable, but they need to be slow-growing, otherwise you will just have to trim the plants instead of the lawn!

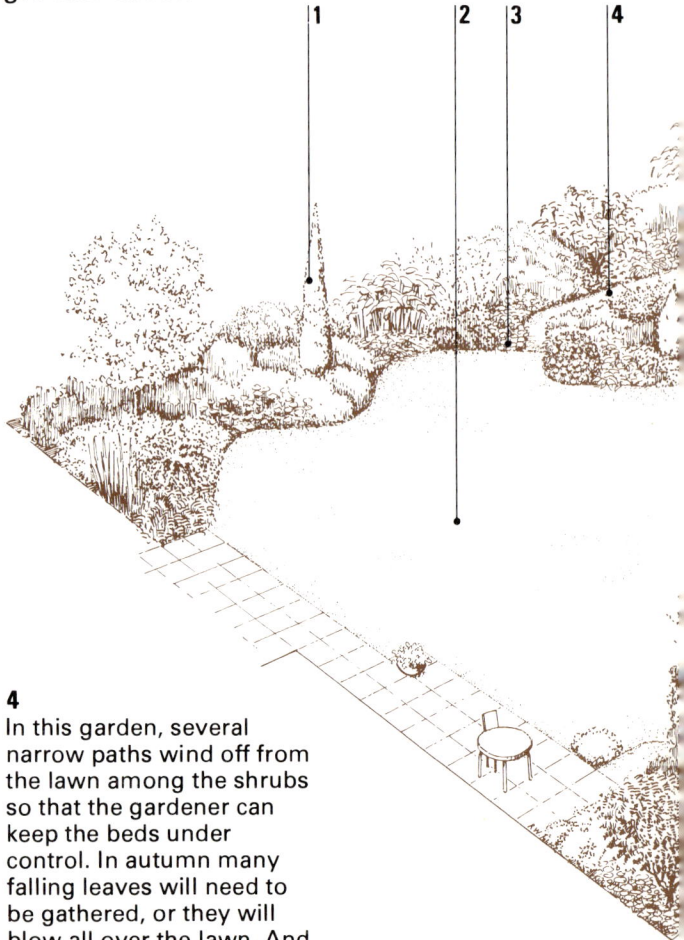

4
In this garden, several narrow paths wind off from the lawn among the shrubs so that the gardener can keep the beds under control. In autumn many falling leaves will need to be gathered, or they will blow all over the lawn. And from time to time the shrubs will need pruning and plants must be fed.

EXAMPLES of TOPIARY
Shapes adapted to any height

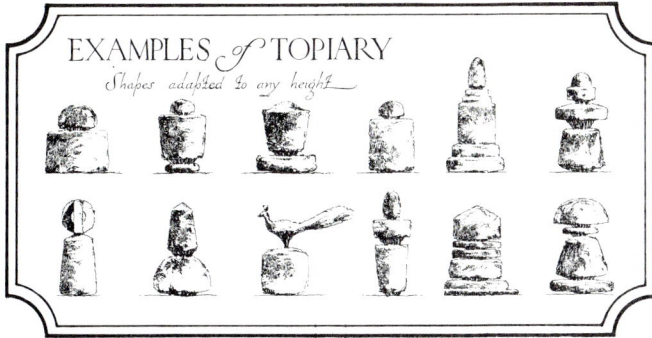

Victorian designs for topiary work are extremely elaborate.

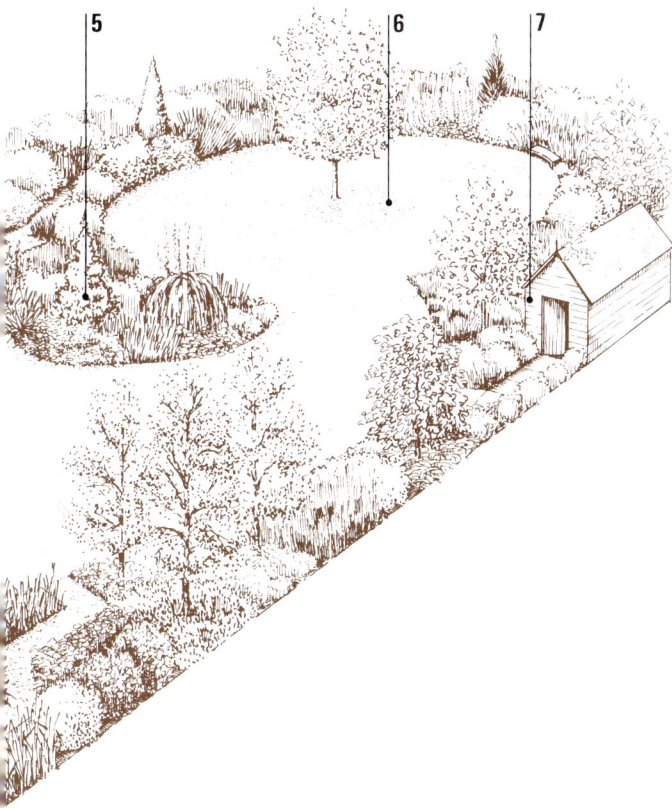

5
Many of the trees and shrubs in our gardens are not in fact native plants, but have been imported from all over the world. Many rhododendrons that flourish in our woods are from the Himalayas, and the eucalyptus comes from Australia. Such plants are often quite hardy, but some may need protection in a very severe winter.

6
If you have a large area of garden with many trees, you may find it worth while to buy a mechanical leaf sweeper. Otherwise, some energetic work with a besom will have the same effect, and you can lift the piled leaves with two boards afterwards. Damp leaves can be very slippery on paths, and may cause an accident.

7
A garden shed is very necessary, but can be hidden away behind trees or bushes. Hidden away somewhere you must have space for an occasional bonfire, and also for a compost heap. In the shed you can keep all your tools, including in this case a large lawn-mower.

Lawns

Lawns are a traditional feature of gardens and do not require a great deal of care if the land has been properly prepared in the beginning. Plan your lawn according to the type of function you would like it to fulfil, decorative or recreational, and remember that although curved shapes are more interesting, more edging work is involved to keep the lawn looking tidy. Take care at the start to remove debris, level the site (pages 28–9) and check drainage (see pages 24–5); hours put in at this stage will save many later on.

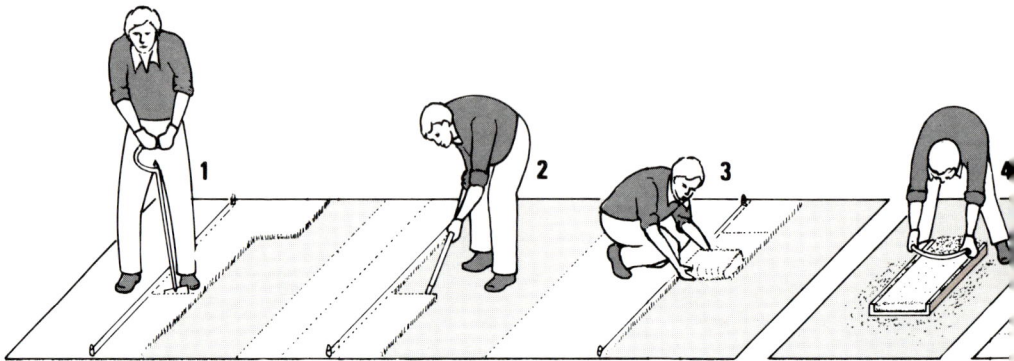

Turf should not be stored for more than a few days before making a lawn. If you can't do the whole job yourself at once, get someone to help or order two small deliveries of turf. If you have to store it, open it out in daylight and keep it damp.

Turfing
1 Cut turves in strips 3 ft (1 m) by 1 ft (30 cm) and 1½–2½ in (3–5 cm) thick, using an edging iron.
2 Lift turf with spade.
3 Roll turf carefully, keeping the soil intact.
4 Level the turf if necessary, by placing in a shallow trough grass side down, and paring off excess soil with a scythe.

5 When laying turf, stagger the joints to prevent turves from lifting up.
6 Beat turf down with a spade to bring it into close contact with the soil.
7 Brush in soil to fill gaps.
8 Apply weedkiller after a few weeks, if necessary.
9 Grass can be cut after it has grown sufficiently.

Seeding
1 Apply weedkiller 1–2 weeks before digging.
2 Clear debris with a rake.
3 Turn the soil with a fork to a depth of 9 in (22 cm).
4 Apply fertilizer.
5 Give the soil a final raking.
6 Test the level of the site, and adjust by further raking or adding topsoil.
7 Sow grass seed.

8 Protect against birds with netting or other methods.
9 Rake off twigs and any small stones after germination.
10 Give the lawn its first cut with a sharp mower when the grass is 1½–2 in (3–4 cm) high.

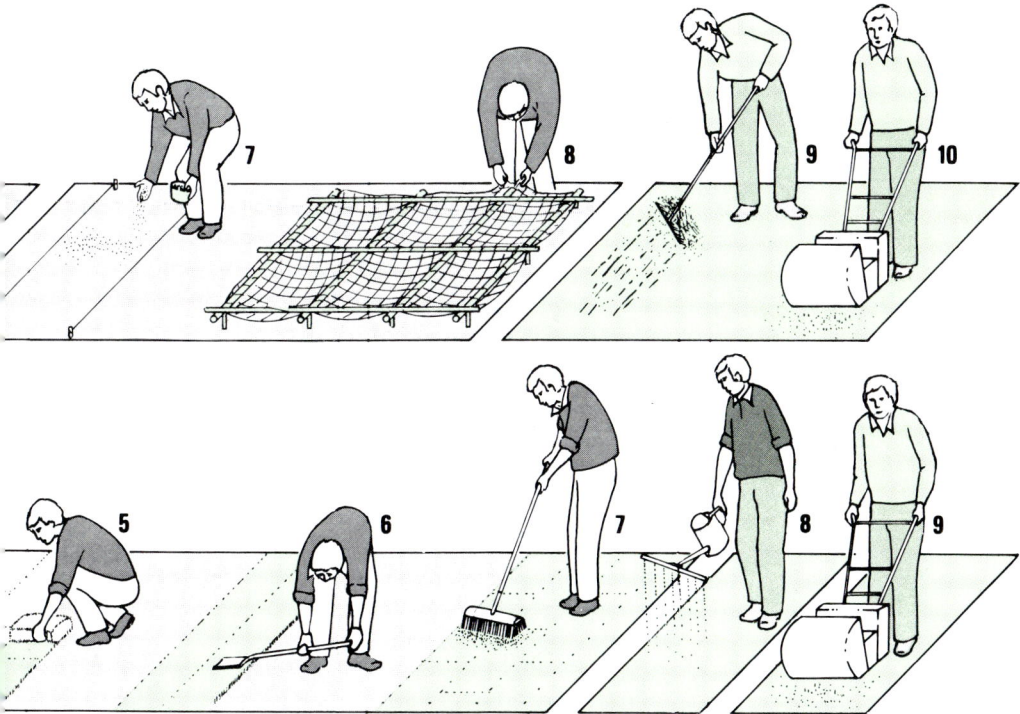

A good lawn is made up of a mixture of different sorts of grass, including festuca, agrostis and poa. Many different seed mixtures are sold; it is advisable to choose a ryegrass-free combination. Allow about 2 oz (56 g) of seed mixture to each square yard of lawn, erring on the generous side. Sow the seed as evenly as possible over the lawn area; this is easier if the seed is first thoroughly mixed with an equal quantity or more of fine sand. Don't worry too much when a lot of weeds appear before the grass, because many of these will die when you start to mow your new lawn.

If you have to make a lawn on very poor, rough land (eg a new plot covered with builders' rubble), use a clover-mix grass seed. The clover will provide some nitrogen, which improves the soil so that the grass can grow. Eventually the grass will take over, when you have cut the lawn a number of times.

Unless the lawn is to be used for ball games, a reasonable amount of maintenance will produce a healthy and attractive stretch of grass. The most important operation of all in lawn care is undoubtedly mowing, but lawns will not grow in perfect condition if this is all that is done to maintain them. Weeds and pests should be controlled and the lawn must be fed and watered, as grass draws a high proportion of nutrients from the soil. Edging gives a good finish.

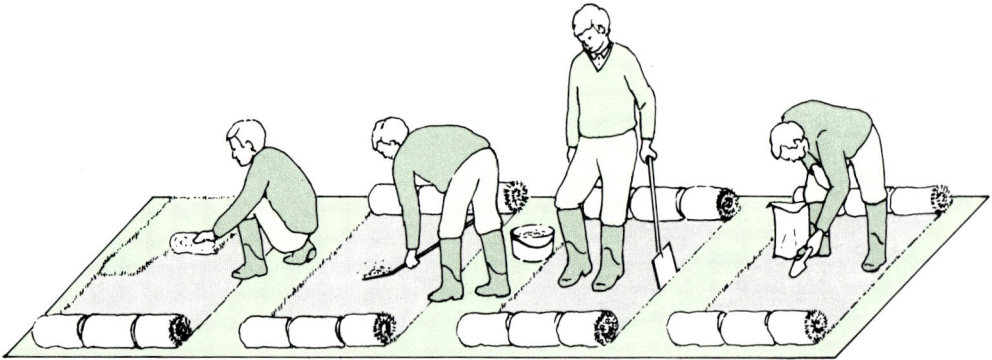

Left: Edging can be done with mechanical tools, long-handled shears or a spade. Once in a while, edges should be re-cut, as constant mowing will make the lawn spread.

Above: To correct a bumpy lawn, make an H-cut on the ridge, fold back flaps and take out excess soil. Tread the area over and sprinkle with sand or fine compost. This method can be used to correct hollows in the same way, adding extra soil.

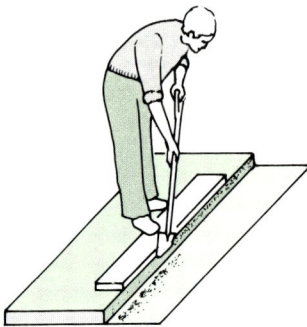

The lawn should be fed at least once a year in the spring with fertilizer. In dry weather, water weekly to keep the grass from going brown. Various sprinklers are available: use one that irrigates a rectangular section, so that it is easy to keep track of the areas that have been soaked.

Buttercups, plantains, daisies, dandelions, moss and other common weeds can be simply controlled by applying selective weedkillers in the summer for maximum effect. Weeding is laborious but may be more efficient if there are fewer patches of larger weeds.

Patches of brown, dying grass may indicate pests such as leatherjackets, cutworms or wireworms, which can be destroyed by the application of various insecticides. Test for leather jackets (a grey grub) by soaking damaged area and covering with polythene. A few hours later the grubs will appear. Fungal diseases cause fine white or pink threads on dying grass.

Rake off leaves, twigs and debris with grass rakes in the autumn. Use two pieces of board to scoop up grass trimmings and put them in a wheelbarrow. A besom is useful for brushing away earthworm casts.

Do not mow grass too closely or weeds may become established in bare patches. A cylinder mower is ideal for a fine finish; rotary mowers are useful for the average garden and should be used once a week in the summer; air-cushion mowers are most practical for slopes.

Shrubs

When choosing a shrub or bush, you should first discover how tall it is likely to become. You may want a tall bush to hide an eyesore, or a low one to grow under – not across – a window. Your choice may be to provide colour in the garden during winter, with an evergreen shrub. Or you may plant a thick bush or two to form a hedge. Some families of plants have very different members: various cotoneasters reach heights from 2–15 ft (60 cm–5 m). Be careful to choose the right one.

Untrimmed single shrubs will probably reach the following heights:
Cotoneaster horizontalis 2–4 ft (0.6–1.2 m)
Daphne 2–5 ft (0.6–1.5 m)
Camellia 3–5 ft (1–1.5 m)
Spiraea 5–6 ft (1.5–1.8 m)
Berberis 6–10 ft (1.8–3 m)
Philadelphus (mock orange) 8 ft (2.4 m)
Ribes (flowering currant) 8 ft (2.4 m)
Buddleia alternifolia 10–12 ft (3–3.6 m)
Jasminum to 15 ft (4.6 m)
Crataegus (hawthorn) 15 ft (4.6 m)
Magnolia soulangeana 20 ft (6 m)
Rhododendron to 40 ft (12 m)
Ilex (holly) to 50 ft (15 m)

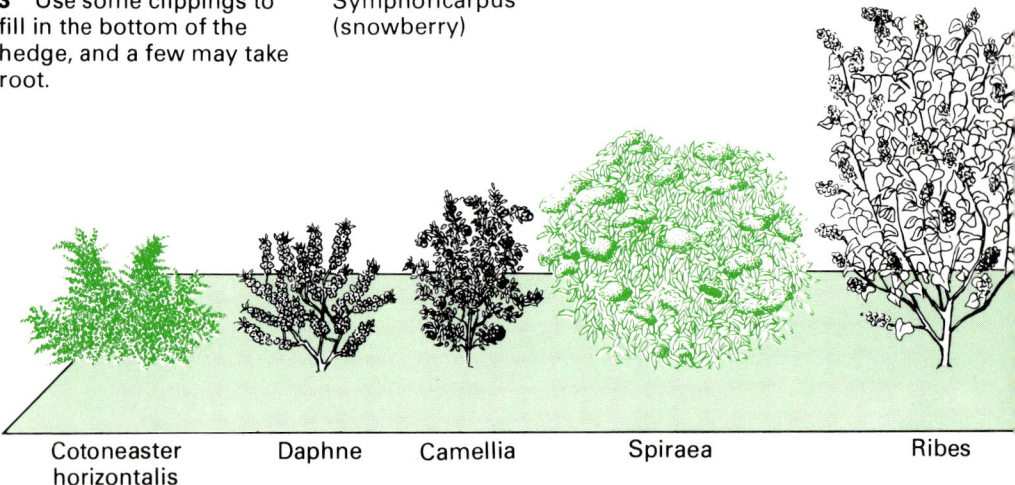

Shrubs are planted close together to form a hedge.
1 The soil near the hedge will be poor, because it has to support a number of strong shrubs; choose undemanding plants to grow there. **2** Cut an established hedge twice a year, in spring and August.
3 Use some clippings to fill in the bottom of the hedge, and a few may take root.

Shrubs for hedges
Berberis
Chaenomeles
Cornus alba sibirica
Cotoneaster
Crataegus (hawthorn)
Fagus (beech)
Lonicera nitida
Prunus laurocerasus (laurel)
Pyracantha
Symphoricarpus (snowberry)

Cotoneaster horizontalis   Daphne   Camellia   Spiraea   Ribes

If your shrub has its roots wrapped in hessian, you simply place the container in a hole and fill in the soil around it. This can be done at any time of year except during flowering. If the shrub has been dug up, however, the roots will have been disturbed; in this case deciduous trees should be moved during the winter.

Evergreens should be moved in spring, around April. Disturb the roots and the soil around them as little as possible. Dig a hole large enough to allow the roots to spread out, and prepare the soil with compost or fertilizer. Put the roots in place gently, and spread the soil over the roots, firming down as you go. Water thoroughly.

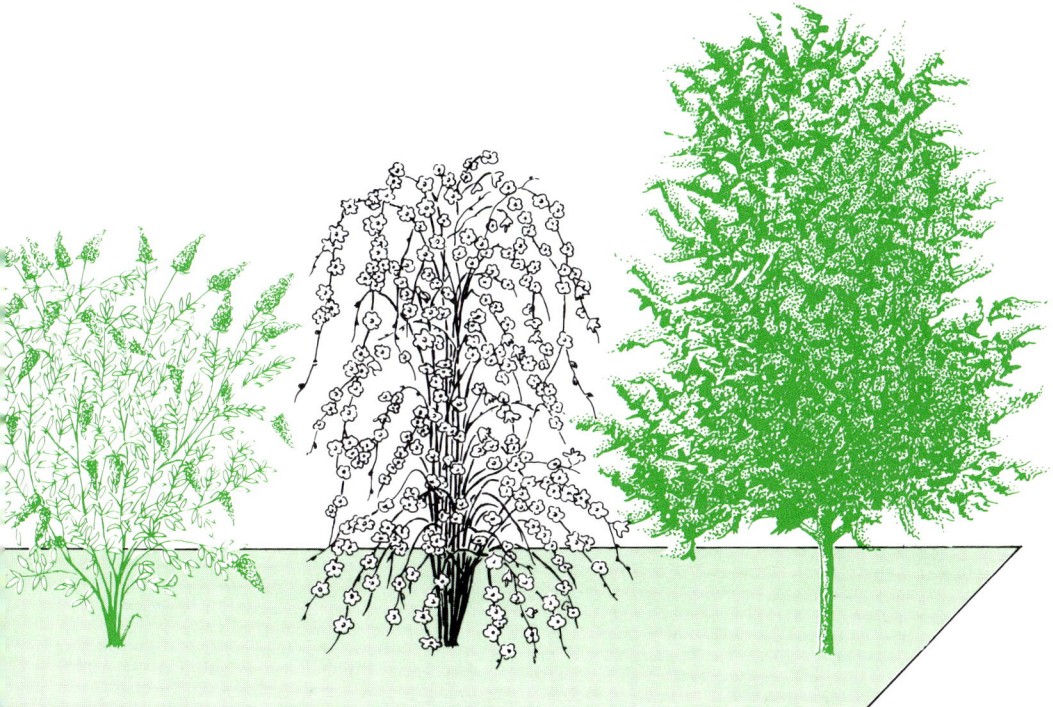

Buddleia alternifolia   Jasminum   Crataegus

Trees

When planting a tree, make sure that it is suitable for its location, and will remain suitable. Its rate of growth will vary with the type of soil, climate, aspect and amount of light available. Some trees (eg Douglas fir, larch) grow very tall, although they may take 100 years to reach full height. Yew trees grow slowly, and never become very tall, but they do spread out sideways. Never plant a large tree too near the house or it will darken the rooms and block the gutters with leaves if deciduous, and its roots may undermine the building. If you have small children, find out which trees have poisonous berries.

Most people plan ahead for about 10–15 years. In 15 years your new tree will have reached the following height:
Juniper 10 ft (3 m)
Holly 10 ft (3 m)
Yew 12 ft (3.6 m)
Oak 25 ft (7.6 m)
Poplar 30 ft (9 m)
Weeping willow 30 ft (9 m)
Silver birch 30 ft (9 m)
Douglas fir 40 ft (12 m)

Juniper   Holly   Yew   Oak

r   Weeping willow   Silver birch   Douglas fir

A paved garden

This garden contains a large area of paving of various kinds, and for this reason it is very easy to maintain, so it would be suitable for a busy family with little leisure for gardening, or for elderly people with limited energy. To lay out such a garden would be rather expensive, but if a small area is done at a time, to a careful overall plan, the work and the costs can be spread over several years.

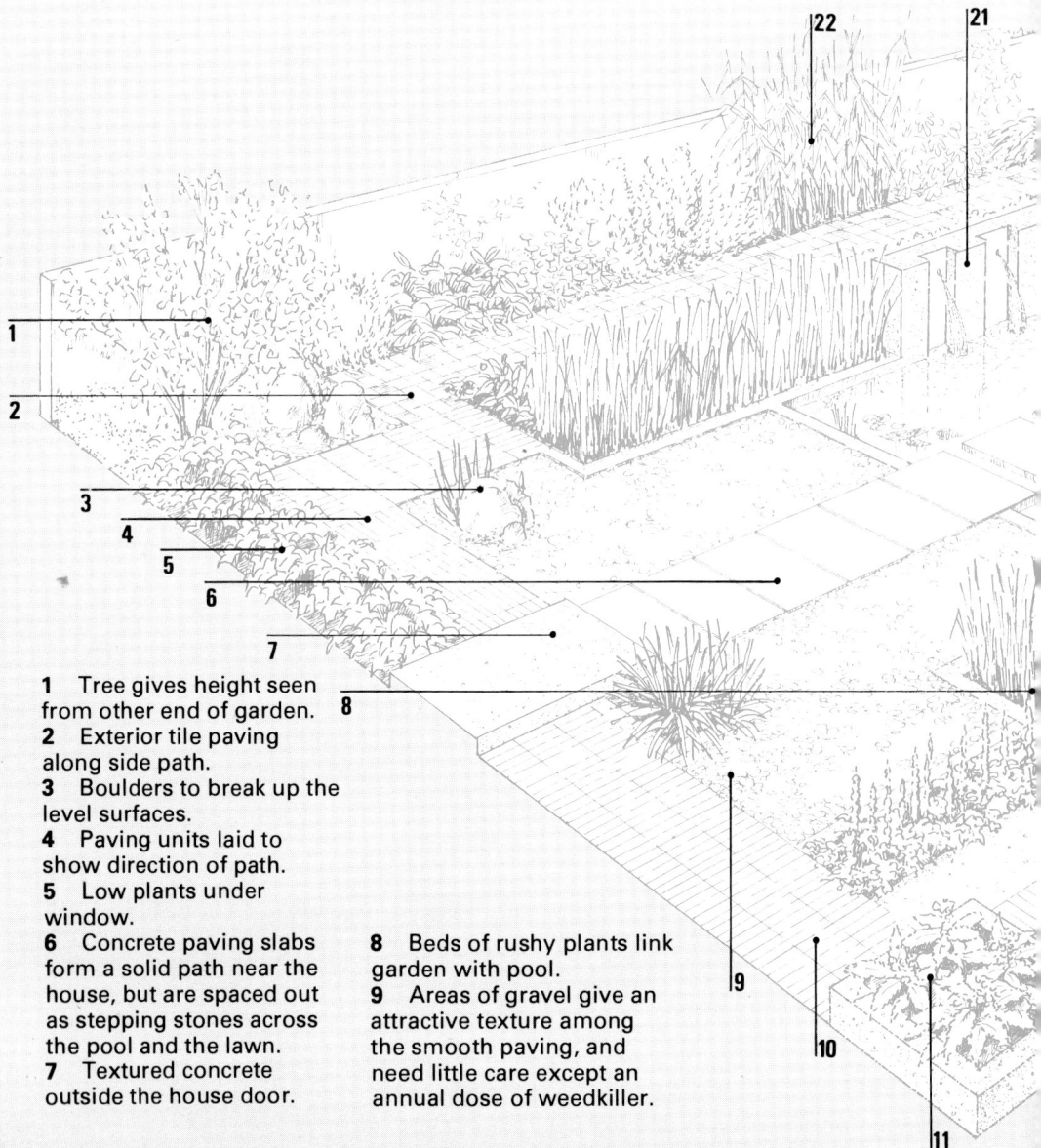

1 Tree gives height seen from other end of garden.
2 Exterior tile paving along side path.
3 Boulders to break up the level surfaces.
4 Paving units laid to show direction of path.
5 Low plants under window.
6 Concrete paving slabs form a solid path near the house, but are spaced out as stepping stones across the pool and the lawn.
7 Textured concrete outside the house door.

8 Beds of rushy plants link garden with pool.
9 Areas of gravel give an attractive texture among the smooth paving, and need little care except an annual dose of weedkiller.

10 An area of bricks or small paving units, laid longways, leads the eye up the garden.
11 Annual bedding plants in a raised bed are easy for an elderly person to manage.

17 Trees at either corner frame the statue and give height at the corners of the garden.
18 Modern statue placed at the garden's focal point.
19 Small paved utility area hidden behind tree and shrubs.

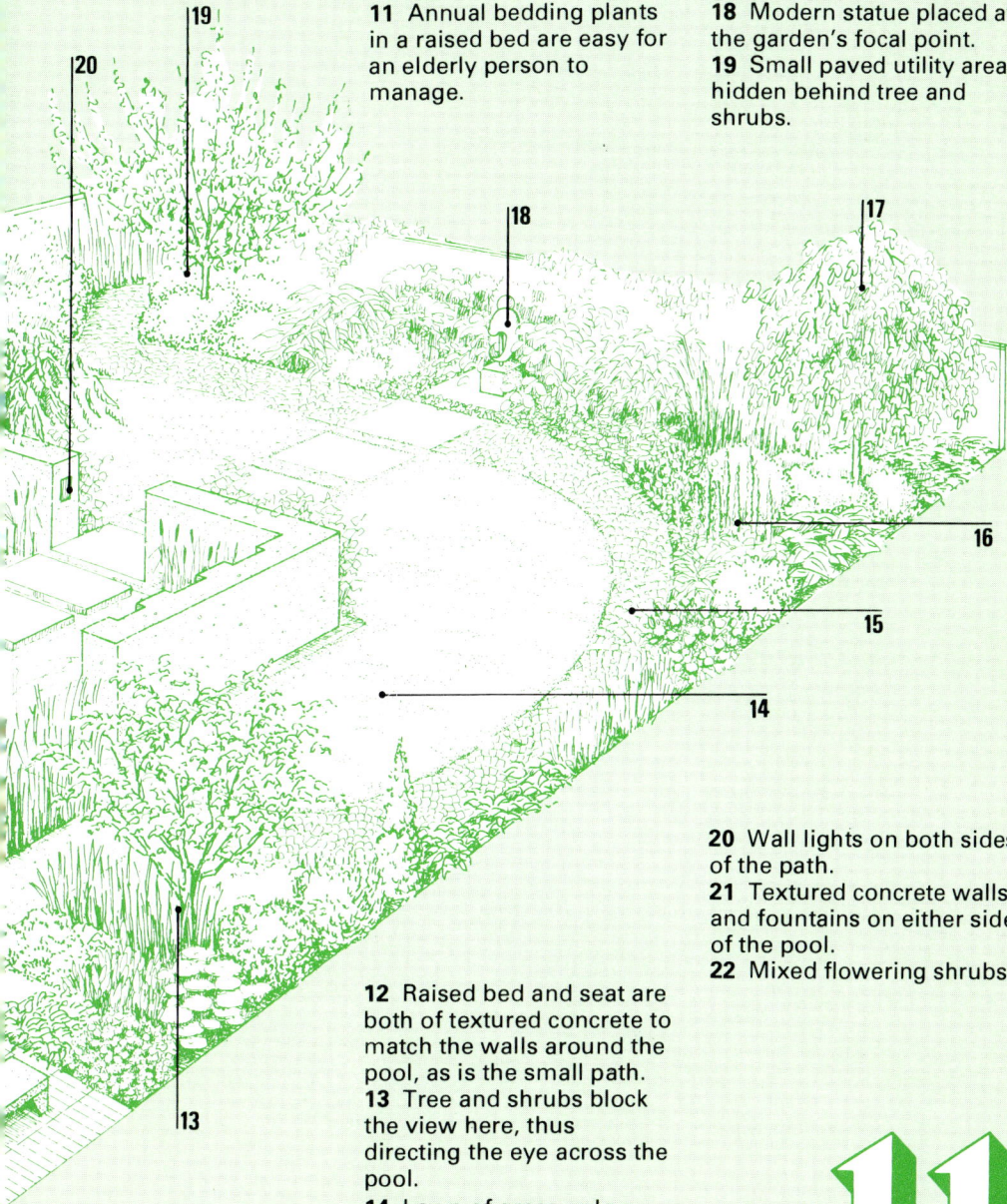

12 Raised bed and seat are both of textured concrete to match the walls around the pool, as is the small path.
13 Tree and shrubs block the view here, thus directing the eye across the pool.
14 Lawn of grass or low plants.
15 Curved path around lawn, of setts, cobbles or flints.
16 Flowers.

20 Wall lights on both sides of the path.
21 Textured concrete walls and fountains on either side of the pool.
22 Mixed flowering shrubs.

11

A stepped garden

This garden, built on a slope, includes several paved areas, and would be ideal for an adult family who prefer entertaining to gardening. But the complex paving would need expert advice on the laying of the strong foundations necessary to create a stable and permanent construction, and it would be very expensive. It could also be a dangerous garden for an elderly infirm person, or for a young child. But on a warm summer evening it would be an attractive setting in which to relax with friends.

1 Wall light illuminates pool at night and prevents an unscheduled midnight swim!
2 Low wall and overhanging ornamental tree help to screen dustbins.

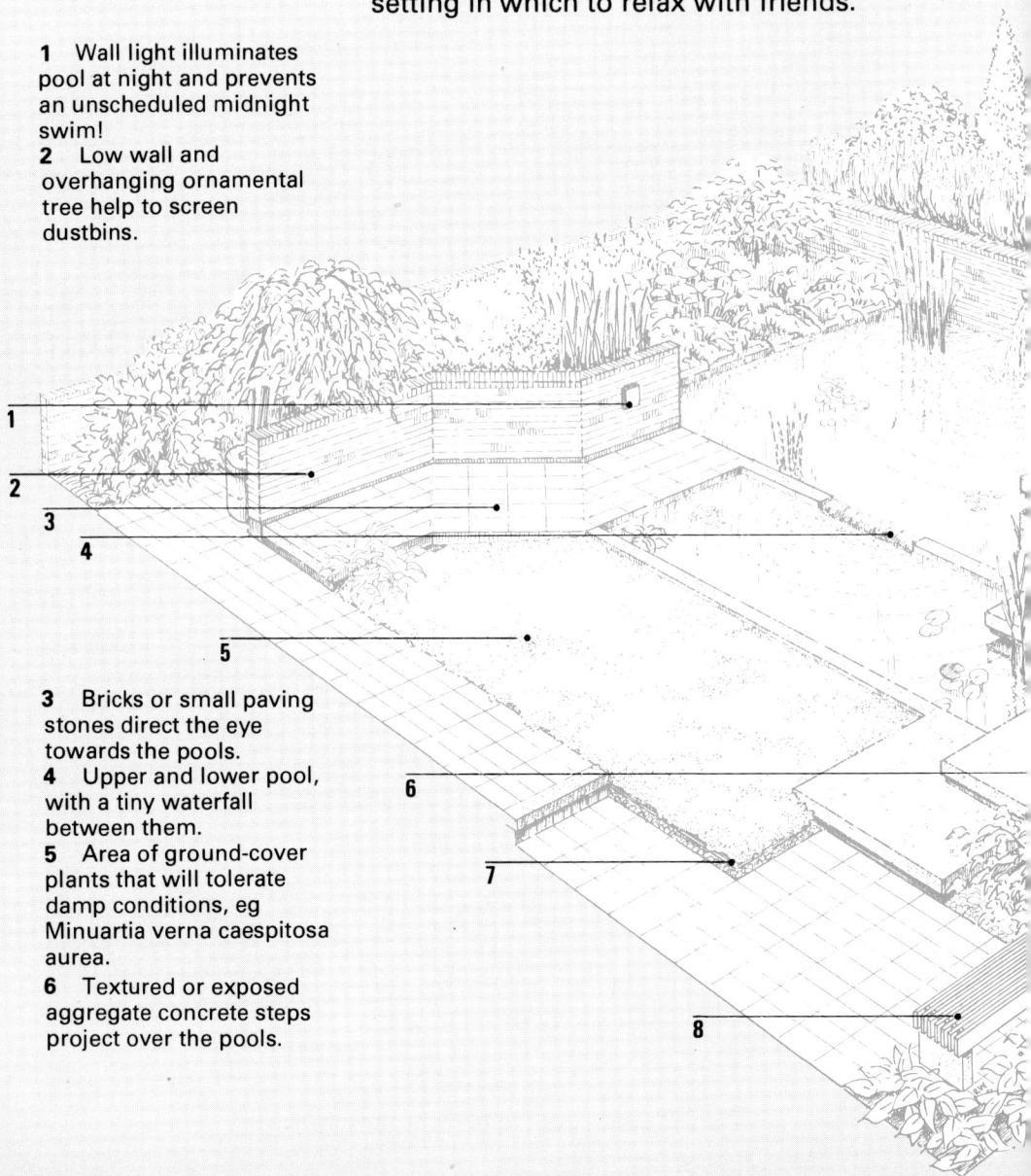

3 Bricks or small paving stones direct the eye towards the pools.
4 Upper and lower pool, with a tiny waterfall between them.
5 Area of ground-cover plants that will tolerate damp conditions, eg Minuartia verna caespitosa aurea.
6 Textured or exposed aggregate concrete steps project over the pools.

7 Water will lie in this lowest area of the garden, but a trench with gravel will solve this problem.
8 A well-situated seat made of timber slats on concrete supports, from which to enjoy the waterfall.

13 Wall light illuminates the steps at night.
14 Roofed sitting area used as shelter from rain or sun.

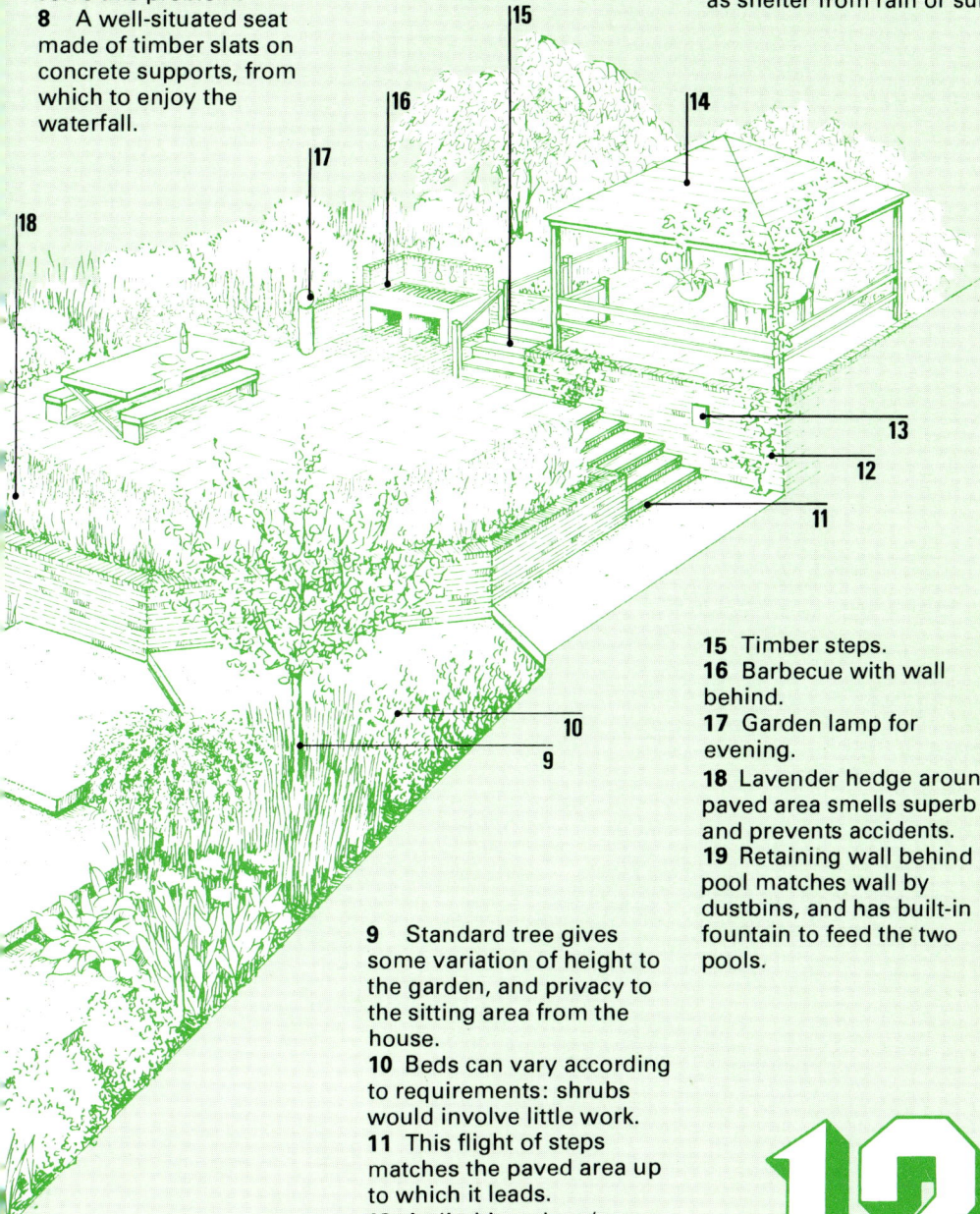

15 Timber steps.
16 Barbecue with wall behind.
17 Garden lamp for evening.
18 Lavender hedge around paved area smells superb and prevents accidents.
19 Retaining wall behind pool matches wall by dustbins, and has built-in fountain to feed the two pools.

9 Standard tree gives some variation of height to the garden, and privacy to the sitting area from the house.
10 Beds can vary according to requirements: shrubs would involve little work.
11 This flight of steps matches the paved area up to which it leads.
12 A climbing plant (roses would be most attractive) softens the geometrical lines of the building, and needs little maintenance.

Paths

Paths are the most expensive part of the garden and may even cost as much as all the other materials and plants put together. They also involve the hardest work and can be quite time-consuming to plan and execute. However, a good path will make a dramatic change in the overall appearance of the garden, giving shape to the design and providing safe and useful walkways from area to area. It is important at the outset to plan all aspects of the path with great care, collecting as much information as

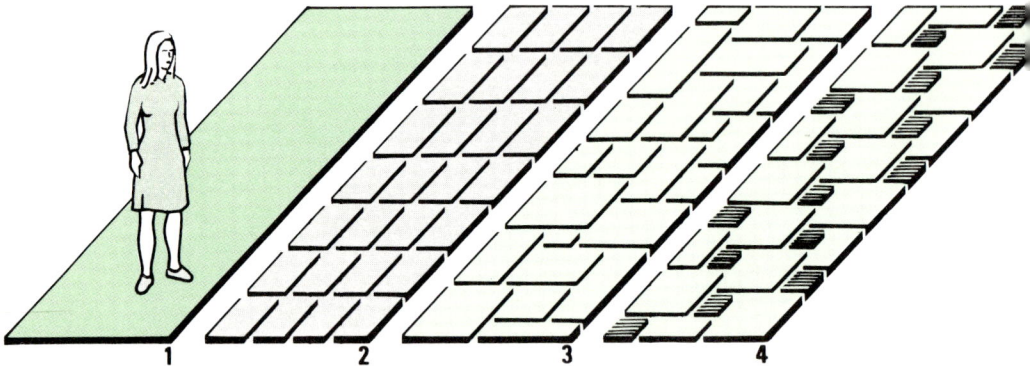

Types of surface and pattern

1 Concrete can be coloured, or the aggregate can be exposed by watering and lightly brushing the concrete several hours after laying.

2 Grid pattern of pre-formed slabs needs careful alignment.

3 Natural stone is expensive, but local varieties may cost less. It has a mellow quality but may be slippery when wet.

4 Mixing artificial and natural stone can cut the cost and give interesting patterns.

5 Pre-cast slabs come in a variety of shapes and colours.

6 Concrete can be scored when damp.

7 Crazy paving should be laid with straight edges at the side.

8 Beach pebbles set in concrete for cobbled effect.

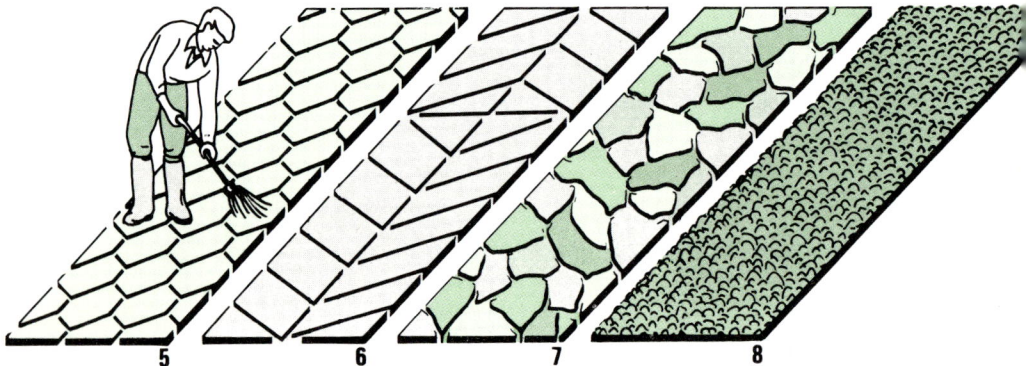

possible on materials and cost, and marking out with string where the path should go. Decide what to do with the soil you will remove to make the foundation, and look at the location carefully to see if the land slopes. There are many types of paving material, which vary a great deal in cost, appearance and technical characteristics. It is a good idea to consider the style of the garden and choose paving that is suitable. This will affect the end result almost as much as skilful laying of the stone itself.

Bricks (above)
Bricks are adaptable due to their size and can be used for corners and edges. They are free-draining, but avoid soft types which crumble in the frost. Set in mortar or on a bed of sand and ashes, laying bricks on side for strength. Brick paths can be made in many attractive patterns.

Features and defects
(below)
1 Edges in wood or stone give strength to a path and make it easy to maintain. Without edging, paths may be overgrown or broken down more easily. But make sure that rainwater can run off.
2 Irregular paving can accommodate random beds of plants or areas of

different materials, eg cobbles.
3 Inadequate foundation or wrong use of path for heavy traffic can cause cracks, which cannot be rectified except by relaying the entire area.
4 Ensure good grouting on paths set in mortar, or weeds may take hold in cracks and disturb the setting of the stones.

1   2   3   4

Most paving materials are surfaces designed to be laid over a solid foundation. The foundation should be dug to a slightly greater depth than the thickness of the paving material, filled with rubble and covered with a layer of bedding sand. Laying concrete paths is not difficult, but involves hard work. The commonest faults arise from poor preparation of the foundation and bad mixing of the ingredients. Other types of paving may need solid foundations by being set in mortar, or a bed of sand and ashes may suffice.

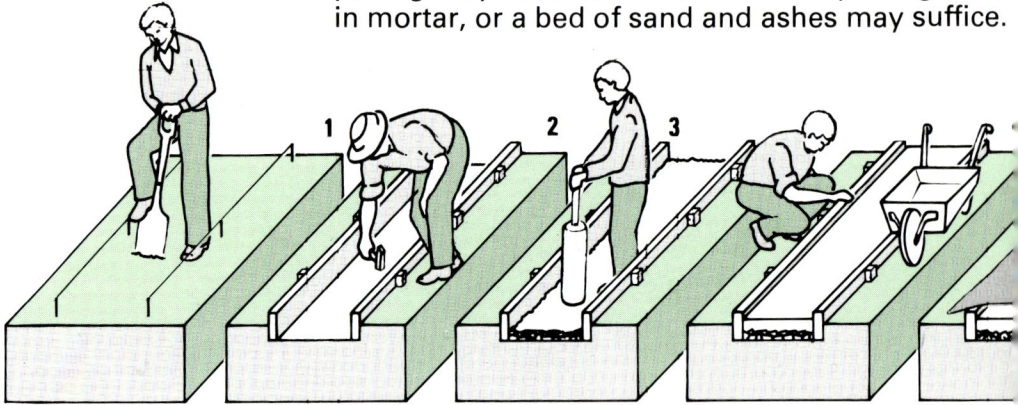

Brick path (below)
1   Mark out the path with string and dig foundation.
2   Lay one edge first, setting bricks on cement bed. Draw the cement up both sides. Leave to set.
3   Place the bricks in a pattern on a 2 in (5 cm) bed of sand, with ⅜ in (1 cm) between them.

4   Tamp the bricks down firmly and check level.
5   Lay the second edge in cement.
6   Brush sand into the joints until all gaps are filled. Fill gap near edge with cement.

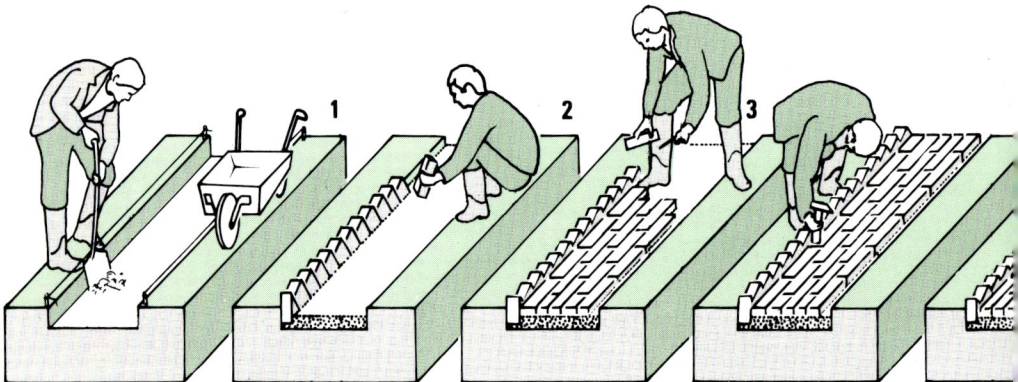

Concrete path
1 Mark out path with string. Dig foundation.
2 Build the mould (shuttering) by placing support posts at intervals and nailing planks to them. Ensure the tops are level.
3 Lay down a rough core of broken bricks and stones. Ram them together.

4 Lay first concrete layer. Tamp surface flat but do not smooth over.
5 In hot weather, cover with sacks and leave 4 days. In cold weather, protect with double layer of polythene.
6 Final layer of concrete. Insert expansion boards in long paths every 2 metres.

7 Pat the surface level with a board as you draw off the surplus, filling in any holes that appear.
8 Use a trowel to smooth and cover again.
9 Remove shuttering after 4–5 days; no heavy wear for a month (until concrete is fully set).

Edging (below)
1 Concrete edging gives strong definition but is almost impossible to move.
2 Brick or stone edging provides attractive contrast.
3 Edging with wood is expensive and wood must be painted with preservative to prevent rotting.

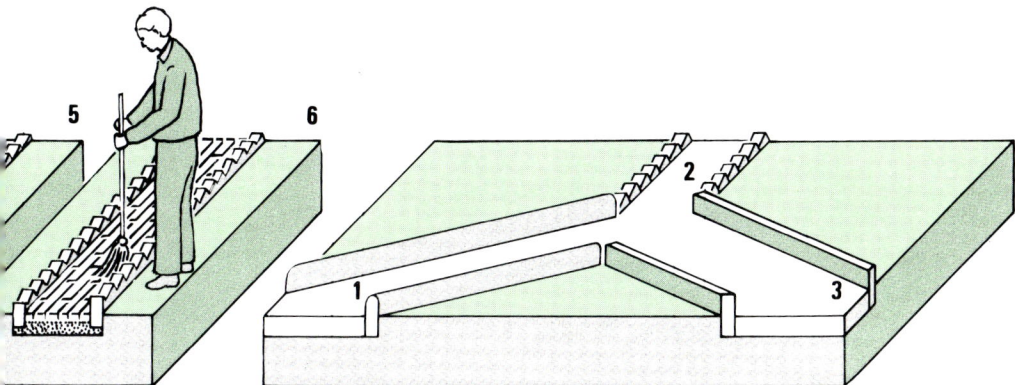

Steps

Many gardens have sloping areas where steps could provide an attractive and useful addition. Begin with steps set in an earth base, which are simple to construct and easy to alter. Solid cast-concrete steps are also fairly easy to make, but may be rather obtrusive. Design the steps so that the depth of each tread plus twice the height of the riser equals 26 in (66 cm). This will give a comfortable flight of steps, no matter what the angle of the slope.

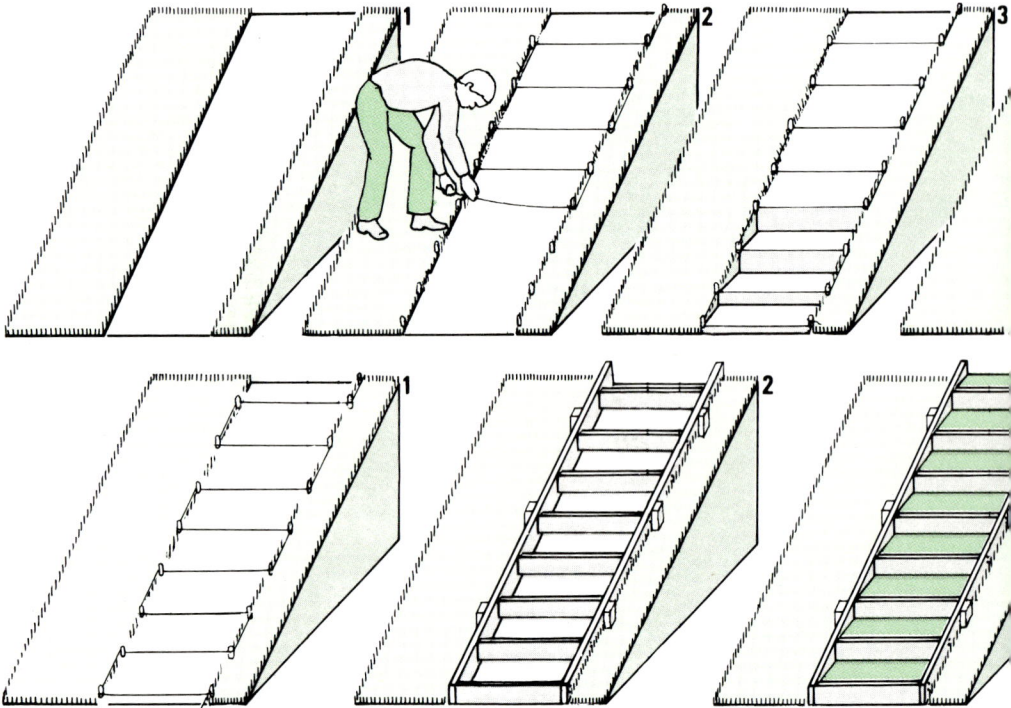

Cast-concrete steps

1 Level the slope and mark out in equal divisions with pegs.

2 Construct shuttering, nailing boards to support posts. Add cross-boards so that all but the lowest have 2 in (5 cm) of space beneath, and the upper edges are level with the lower edges of the one above. (See cross-section.)

3 Shovel cement behind each cross-board.

4 Tamp concrete flat.

5 After 4–5 days remove the shuttering and fill the riser faces with a mix of concrete and water.

6 Build a brick edge around the steps to help integrate them into the garden.

Block steps
1 Level the slope.
2 Mark out the slope, dividing it equally with pegs placed opposite each other about 20 in (51 cm) apart. String the pegs together. The pegs should be level with each other.
3 Dig backwards, level with each cross string, taking out soil. Dig downwards for risers.

4 Begin with bottom step (thin cast-concrete slab), laying slab on bed of soil. Press down firmly until level. Tip soil over back of slab.
5 Lay risers (slabs, bricks, blocks) on this soil and bed down.
6 Fill in behind with soil, put another slab on top with the edge protruding.

7 Brush away surplus earth and continue to the end of the flight of steps. This method can be used with a cement foundation to give extra strength. Allow an extra 2 in (5 cm) of depth and proceed as before.

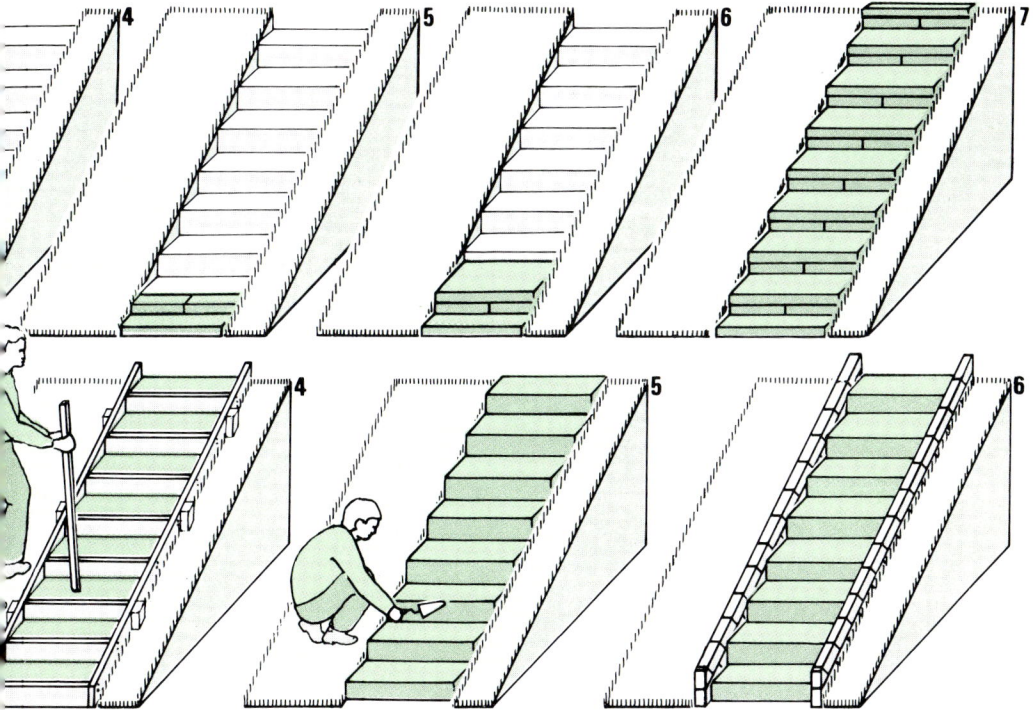

Cross-section of the steps, showing riser (**a**) and tread (**b**).

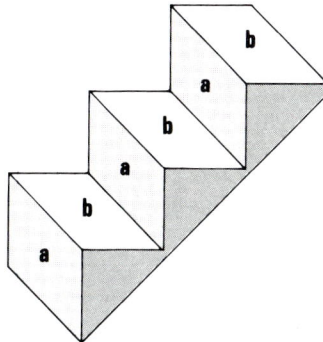

A walled garden

A solid wall gives complete privacy at ground level, and is primarily useful for defining the boundary of the garden. But even a fence with spaces in it gives a suggestion of privacy, and forms a secluded area within the garden. In many parts of the country walls are indispensable as a windbreak, allowing plants to flourish that would otherwise die. Walls also hide unsightly but necessary parts of the garden. Fences and pergolas support climbing plants.

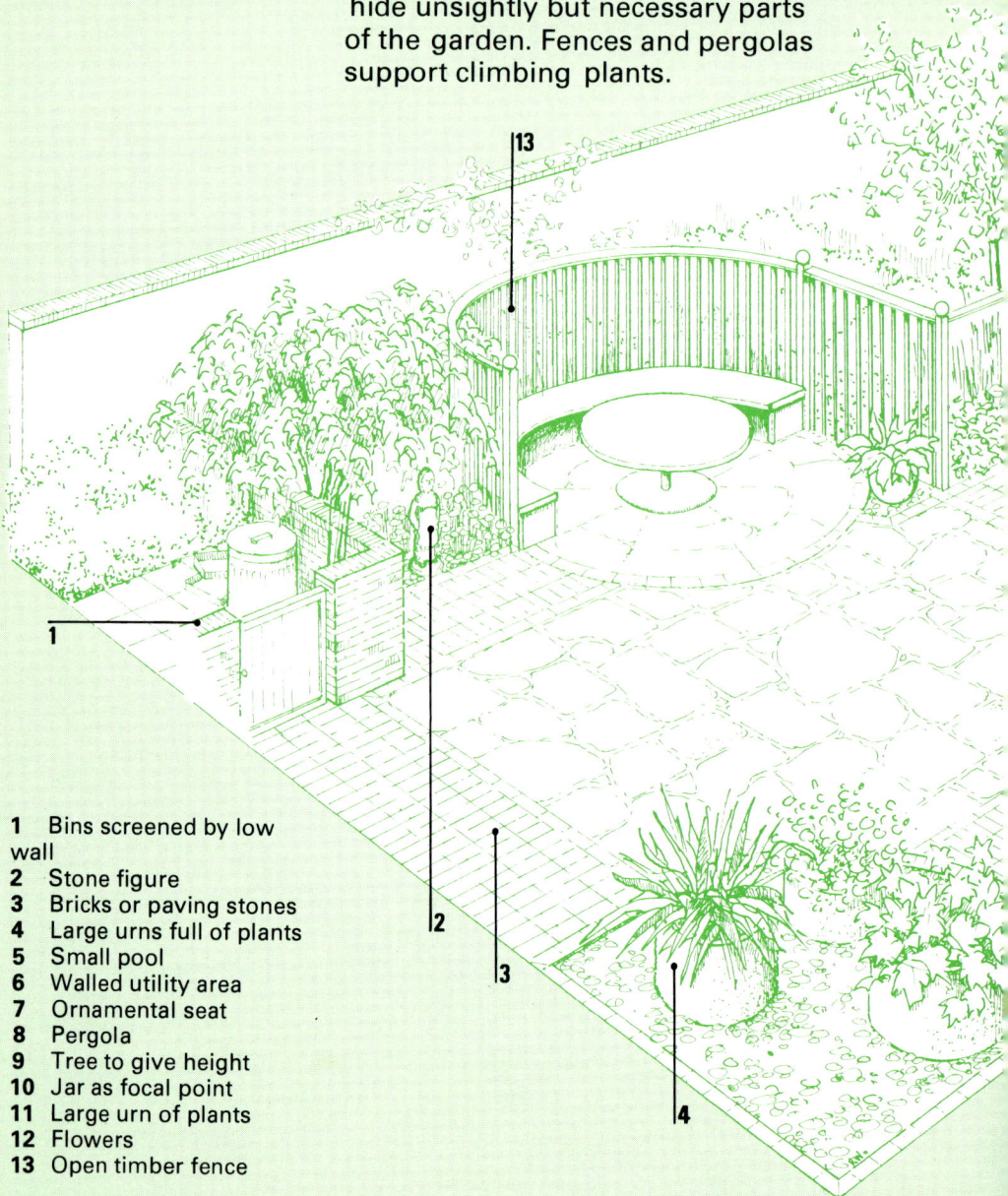

1 Bins screened by low wall
2 Stone figure
3 Bricks or paving stones
4 Large urns full of plants
5 Small pool
6 Walled utility area
7 Ornamental seat
8 Pergola
9 Tree to give height
10 Jar as focal point
11 Large urn of plants
12 Flowers
13 Open timber fence

11

10

9

8

7

6

5

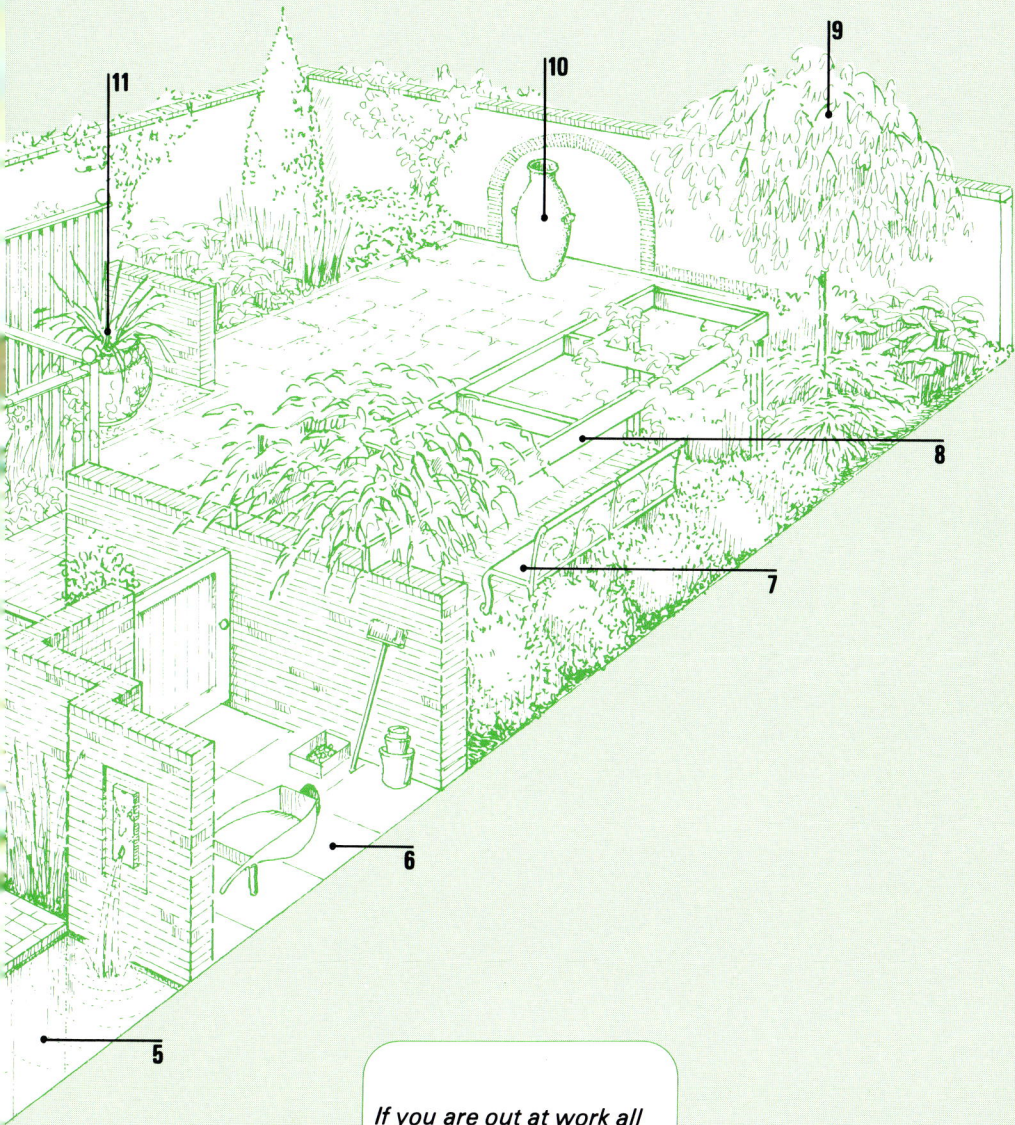

If you are out at work all day, put your seat where it gets evening sunshine (but not straight into your eyes) so that you can enjoy it when you get home on summer evenings.

13

1
The walls are painted white, and capped with warm red bricks that match the colour of the brick paving.

2
A low brick wall surrounds the dustbin area and partly disguises it.

3
Bricks or small paving stones laid lengthwise direct the eye outwards, down the garden.

4
An area of random natural stone looks informal and spacious, and gives relief from the regularity of the bricks.

5
A semi-circular painted or natural timber fence makes a secluded area for meals, and allows the diners to see the plants beyond.

6
Large containers filled with soil are heavy, and can be unstable. To prevent any accidents you must make sure that they are embedded into the surface on which they stand.

7
Beach pebbles set in a bed of mortar act as a good foil to large containers planted with showy annuals or perennials.

Victorian curved seat at the
end of the bowling green.

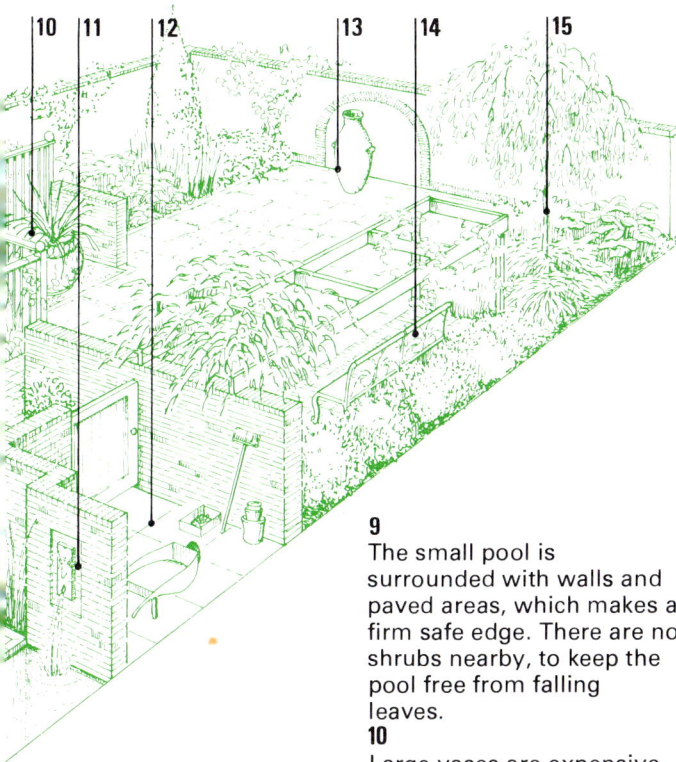

10 11 12 13 14 15

11
The same wall that hides
the utility area also has a
striking carved stone
fountain inset in it, hiding
the mechanism of the water
supply to the pond.

12
A paved walled utility area
is within easy reach of the
whole garden, and provides
a useful place for tools.

13
The large empty jar stands
at the focal point of the
whole garden. Make
sure that you choose one
that is large enough: a jar
that was too small would
look silly.

14
The pergola, which would
look lovely covered with
roses, clematis or
honeysuckle, has a seat
beneath from which to
enjoy it.

15
If you plant very large trees,
their powerful roots may
undermine the walls and
weaken them dangerously
Walls need to be based on
very sound foundations.

9
The small pool is
surrounded with walls and
paved areas, which makes a
firm safe edge. There are no
shrubs nearby, to keep the
pool free from falling
leaves.

10
Large vases are expensive
to buy, but you can often
use other containers for
such arrangements: an old
ornamental chimneypot or
a cast-off car tyre can both
be used for plants.

8
To allow access to the beds
behind the fence, one
section of the fence is
hinged to make a gate.
Even the least demanding
plants need some attention
occasionally.

Garden ornaments

What you put into your garden is a matter of personal taste, and anything *you* like is right. Don't be put off by comments from outsiders, because you are the person who has to live with it. Your choice may be to fill the garden with plants only, or you may pick out several items from a manufacturer's catalogue of ornaments and seats. If you already have ornaments in the garden and just want a change, perhaps you can move them to another corner. Or an old sink, barrel or wheelbarrow can be used as an unusual and inexpensive ornament.

Garden ornaments
1 An old sink or bath can be used for plants or herbs.
2 A barrel looks attractive with strawberry plants or herbs growing in it.
3 Urns give a grand touch, but need watering in dry weather.
4 A statue provides a focal point in a shrubbery.
5 Sundials look attractive in a lawn or rose garden.

Ponds and fountains
There is an enormous range of garden ponds available.
1 A pond can be sunk in the ground, to look natural.
2 An urn-type pond with a surround looks more formal. Fountains sound cool and refreshing in summer; they can be either central 3 or built into a rear wall of rocks 4.

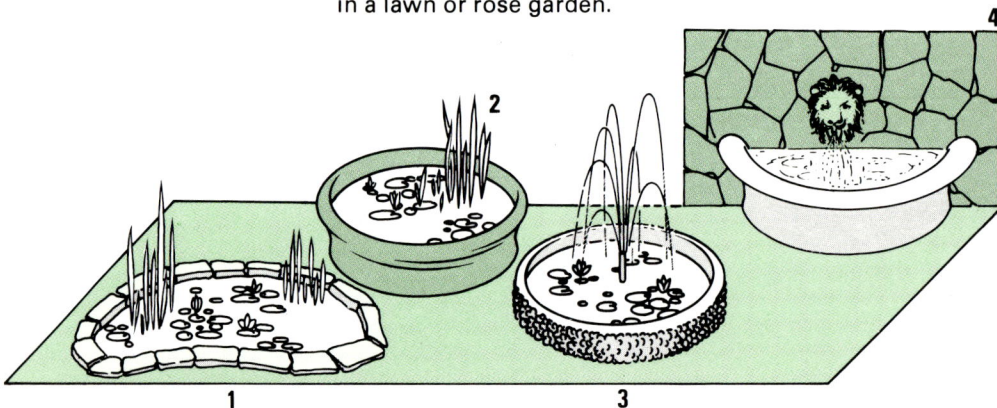

Seats
1 A built-in seat is unobtrusive, but cannot be moved to another place.
2 Wrought-iron seats can sometimes be bought quite cheaply secondhand.
3 Deckchairs are pleasant, but remember to take them indoors afterwards.
4 A seat can be built around a mature tree quite simply.

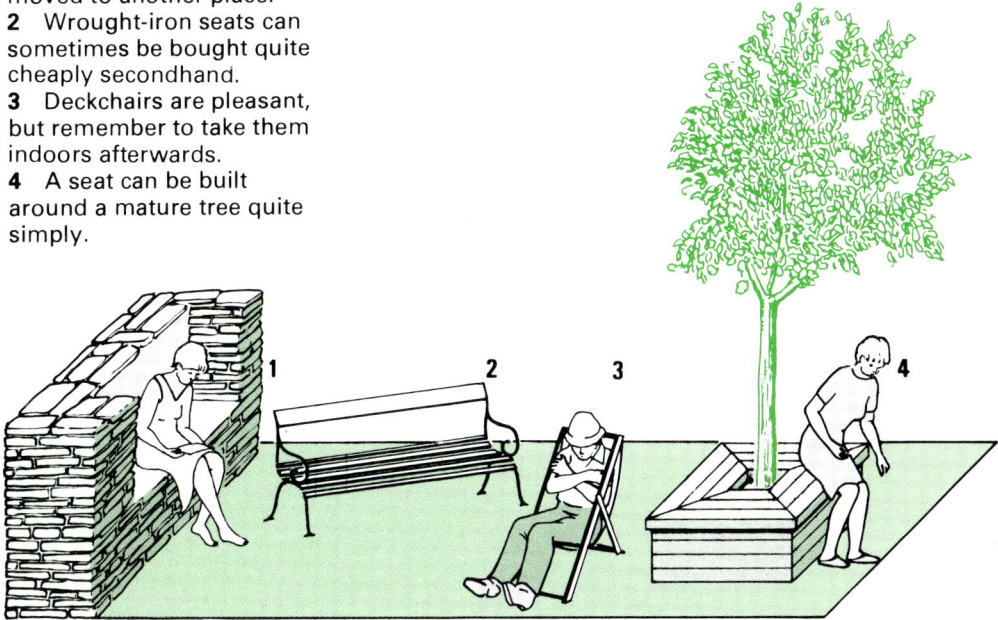

Structures
1 Everyone needs a rubbish bin, but many prefer to hide it behind a wall or hedge.
2 Trellises divide one area of the garden from another.
3 A pergola for climbing roses takes a lot of space, but looks very splendid. A gazebo or summerhouse can be useful in hot weather.

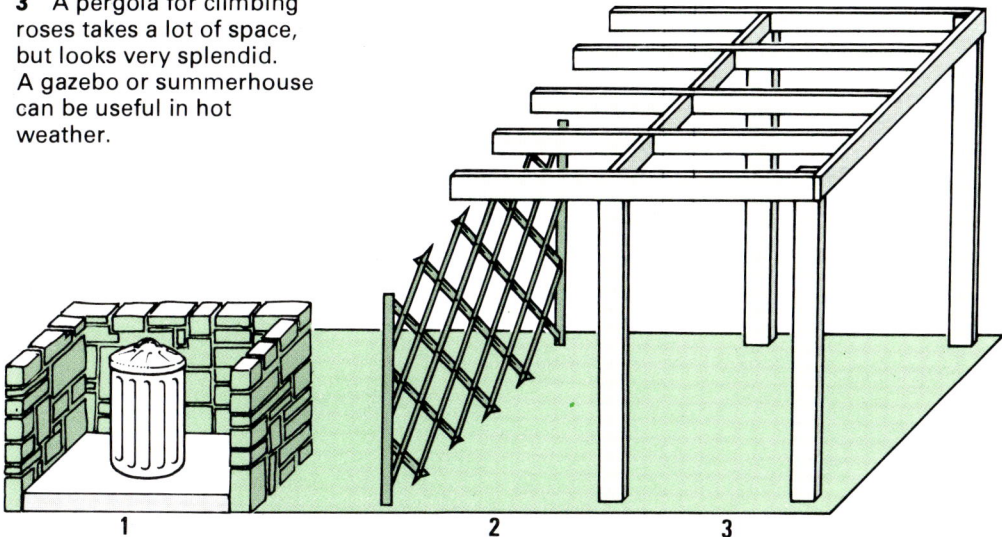

Fences

In a small garden, the fence that is put up as a boundary will always be in view. Bear this in mind when choosing fencing, and consider training climbing plants against the fence if you prefer a more natural look. Fences are usually put up to provide screening, and to be effective they should be anchored firmly and, if wooden, treated often with preservative. Do not underestimate the force of the wind. No part of the fence should touch the ground, except the support posts, which can be timber (treated

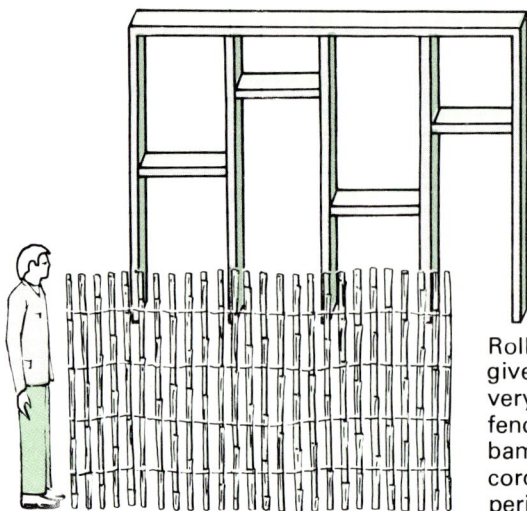

Louvred wooden screen, built on the site. Needs frequent repainting with oil-bound paint or creosote, and may weather badly. Suitable to screen a patio.

Rolls of bamboo screening give privacy, but require very strong supports, as the fence itself is fragile. The bamboo is linked with cords, and these soon perish.

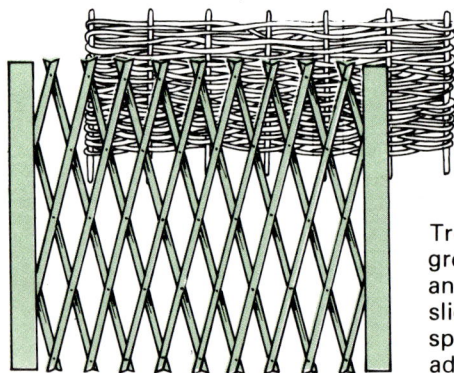

Wattle hurdles fit in well in a rural setting and are an effective windbreak, but they are of fixed length and cannot be divided to fill a shorter space if needed.

Trellis panels are useful for growing climbing plants, and can be expanded slightly to fit a required space, unlike the less adaptable panels opposite.

with preservative) or concrete. Fencing can be built on the site, but it is easier to buy fencing kits or ready-made panels to save wastage. Apart from timber fencing, various types of chain link and plastic fences are also available, but these often need disguising in a home garden, with some kind of climbing plants, or they will be very obtrusive. Plastic fencing varies in colour, and some shades will blend in with their background easier than others, so consider the matter carefully before buying.

A pergola is also a good way of fencing off one area of the garden from another: eg to give some privacy to a swimming pool or to a sitting area or patio.

Close-boarded fencing gives total privacy and can be bought in kit form. It is durable but may need to be treated with preservative.

Interwoven panel may lack strength if it is a cheaper variety, but will last longer mounted on good-quality supports.

Horizontal fencing gives decorative screening and can be used for boundaries. Usually painted, which needs renewing every few years.

Paling is usually 3–4 ft (1–1.2 m) high and is used for front boundaries. Looks best when teamed with cottage-type garden. It is inexpensive and can have a natural or painted finish.

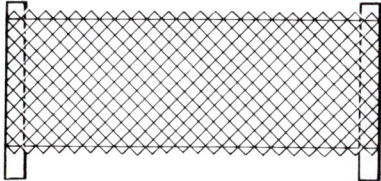

Chain link is fairly cheap and effective as a boundary fence. Plastic-covered wire prevents metal from corroding, but consider the colour of the wire carefully before you buy it.

Walls

Walls are useful for boundaries, terrace edges, to support slopes or to make raised flower beds. The initial cost of constructing a wall is quite high, but they require little maintenance once built, and provide the most effective screening as well as excellent support for plants. Natural stone is used to make dry walls; a variety of man-made and natural materials can be used to build cemented walls. Faced with these

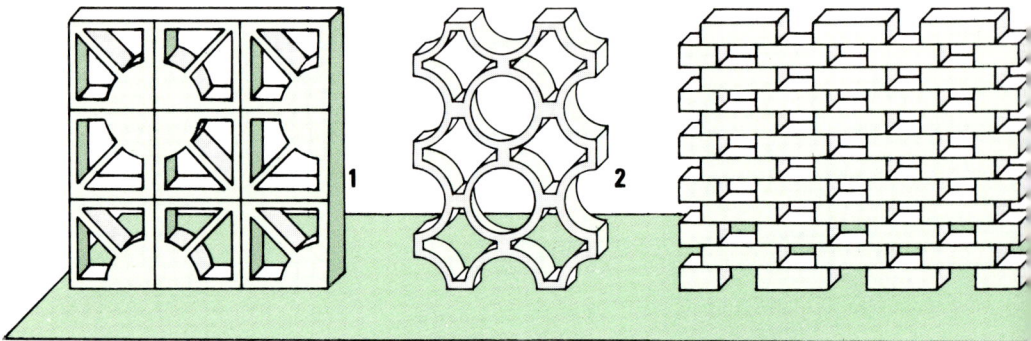

Hollow drystone wall
Drystone walls are made without mortar, usually in natural stone. This hollow wall has a cavity which is used for growing plants.
1   Trench
2   Concrete foundation 3 in (7.5 cm)
3   Drainage holes 2 ft (60 cm) apart made by placing timber plugs in concrete and removing after base has set
4   Large flat foundation stones
5   Rubble for drainage
6   Smaller stones
7   Loam in cavity
8   Cross-ties of stone or iron every 4–5 ft (1.2–1.5 m)
9 Sides slope inward to improve stability.
10 Plants in top of wall cavity and on sides

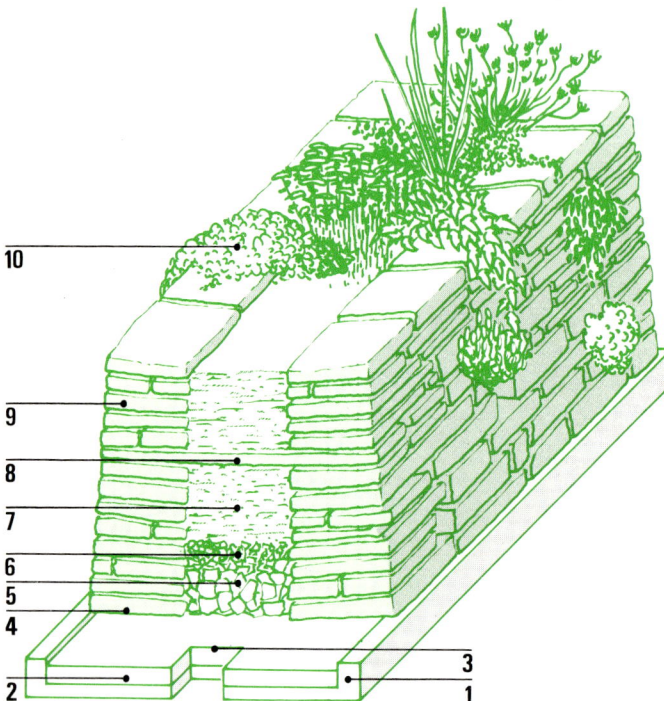

alternatives, the best way to begin is to decide how much you can afford, and then select material in the range that will fit with the style of your garden. Walls have formal lines and give a strong visual impact, especially if they form boundaries. Many types of wall up to medium height are easy to construct, as long as care is taken in alignment, but solid cast-cement walls should never be attempted by the amateur.

Types of wall
1   Pre-cast openwork concrete block in offset pattern makes overall design when laid.
2   Shaped outlines are also useful for light screens.
3   Open brickwork wall.
4   Curved brick wall is actually stronger than a straight wall and gives an interesting effect.

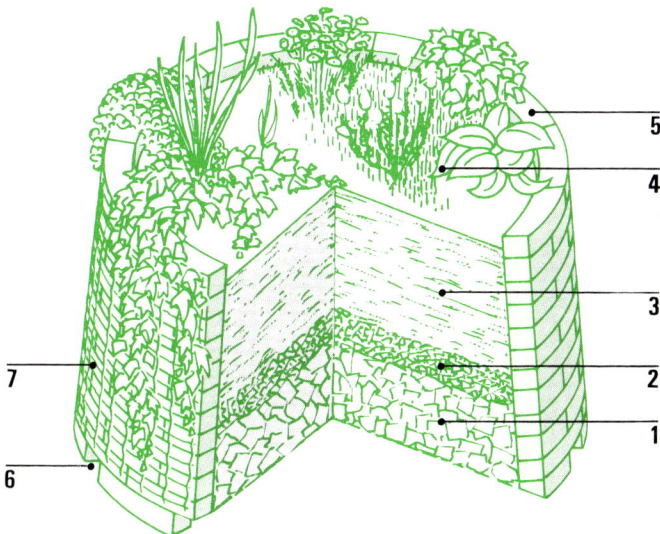

Raised bed
A circular raised flower bed forms an interesting feature and allows older people or invalids to garden without bending over (page 136).
1   Rubble
2   Small shingle
3   Compost or soil mixed with bone meal
4   Flowers or shrubs
5   Cemented walls laid on paving
6   Drainage holes
7   Plastic mesh to encourage creeping plants, eg ivy

Modern pre-cast openwork blocks make good screening walls, combining the strength of an ordinary wall with lightness of appearance. These blocks come in many colours, textures and patterns, and are ideal for hiding utility areas from view without creating a dark yard. These walls should be over 4 ft (1.2 m) high if they are to be effective in screening, and some type of added reinforcement is a good idea. They are easy to build, but need careful alignment.

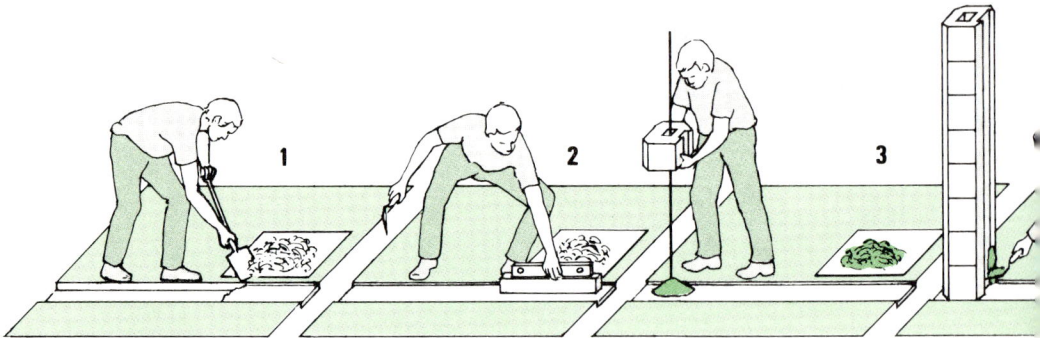

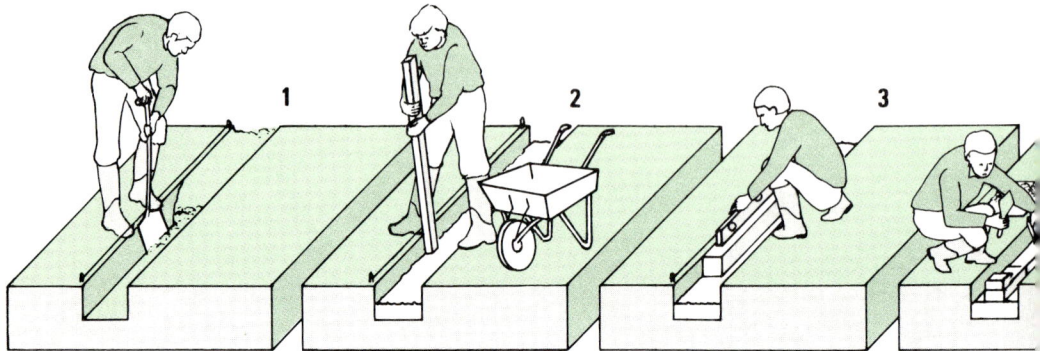

Building a brick wall
1 Dig trench 9 in (23 cm) deep and a bit wider than bricks.
2 Lay 4 in (10 cm) foundation of concrete, keeping sides clean. Ram the concrete down.

3 Make sure concrete is level; leave to set.
4 Spread 4 ft (1.2 m) long layer of mortar at each end and lay first bricks, one at each end. Use guide string to help line up middle bricks.

5 Build up wall at either end, using string to line up. Fill in the middle: cut bricks here if necessary, where it shows least.
6 Also check vertical (see next page).
7 Finished wall.

Building a screen block wall
1 Dig a neat trench 9 in (23 cm) deep and the same width.
2 Lay 4 in (10 cm) foundation of concrete, keeping sides clean. Level concrete down.
3 Lower pillar block onto mortar at base of rod; check for level; fill hole in centre with mortar. Put mortar on top of first block;

repeat the process.
4 Pillar block may have a slot for screen block edge. Put mortar on each corner.
5 Slide screen block into slot. Use a small amount of mortar in vertical joints. Light pressure will set the blocks together.
6 Upper courses must be properly aligned. Check level frequently.
7 Where wall meets

paving, fill any gaps with mortar. Remember that both sides of the wall should be clean.
If you are making a screen block wall, it is often a good idea to start with a low wall (say 1 ft/30 cm) of ordinary bricks, and then to build up the screen blocks from these. This ensures that soil and damp from below will not spoil the effect .

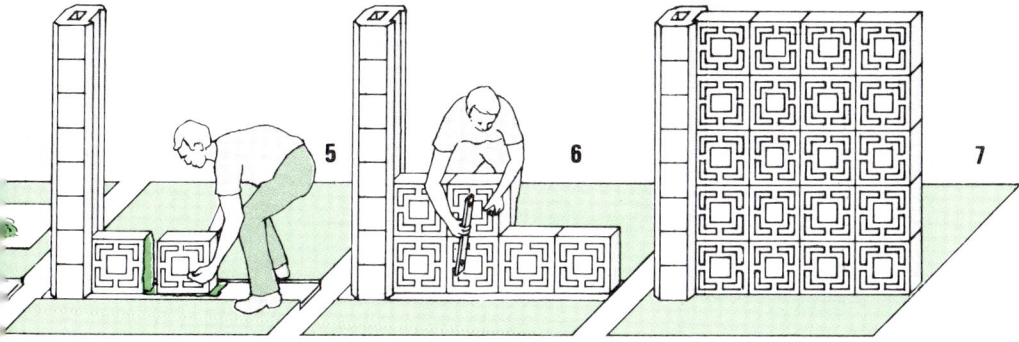

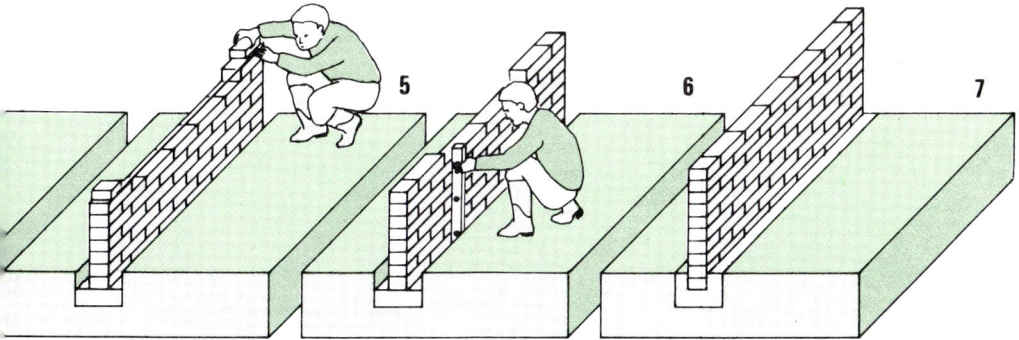

A builders' ordinary spirit level is ideal for checking walls. They should be checked horizontally, vertically and on the rake, holding the level diagonally from the corner block and tapping back any blocks that are out of line.

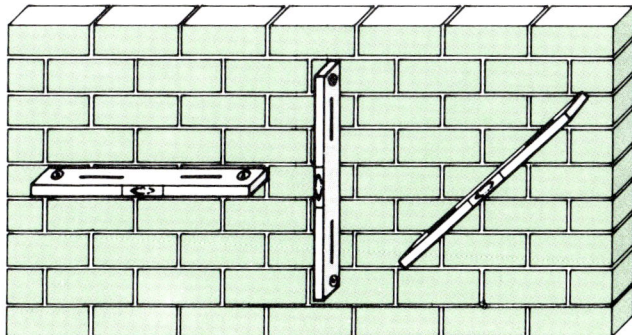

An elaborate garden of
1571; note the beehive, top right.

Chapter four
Purpose-built gardens

The gardens shown in this chapter have all been designed with certain restrictions. In some cases restrictions are the unavoidable ones imposed by necessity: everyone needs somewhere to put (and probably to hide) the dustbin, and most people need a place to hang out the washing. Many people have young children to accommodate and to amuse safely within their gardens, away from the dangers of traffic. Ugly buildings or fittings of some kind often limit the gardener's choice of possible designs. And an increasing number of older house owners have to try to cope with age and perhaps infirmity while running a house and a garden as well. In other cases, the restrictions on garden design are imposed by the owner himself: his garden *must* have several ponds and waterfalls, or it must contain a swimming pool big enough for a really energetic swim. In all these cases, the use of imagination and flair in planning the layout of the garden can make a real difference; and the finished area not only fulfils its purpose, but fulfils it beautifully.

Drawing of a Japanese tea garden, carefully planned.

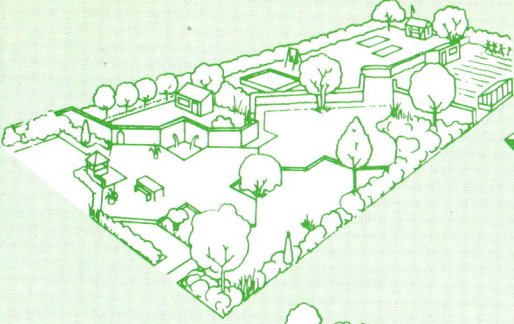

14 This design gives you ideas on layout of certain areas for a particular purpose: a universal need, maybe, or a special personal interest.

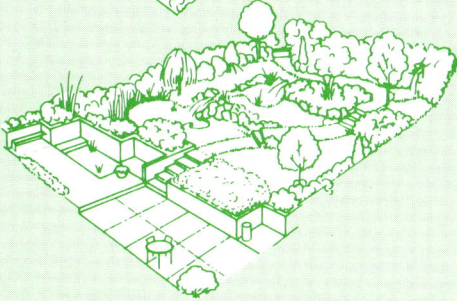

15 This garden is planned for the enthusiast for water in many forms: in still pools, trickling streams, fountains and waterfalls.

16 Swimming pools are nowadays increasingly popular, and many people will welcome a few tips on how to build and position them most suitably.

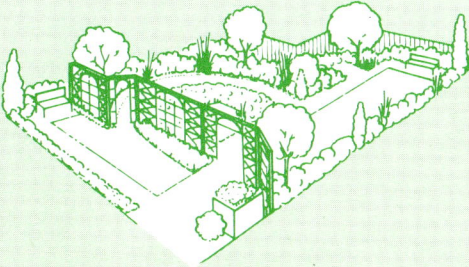

17 Many gardens have some ugly feature that their owner would like to disguise. The design here gives some ideas on how to cope with eyesores.

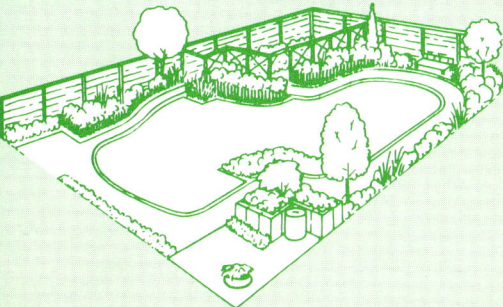

18 Through age, physical handicap or just ordinary laziness, many people want a garden that is easy to maintain and yet attractive to relax in.

A divided garden

This rather large garden has been broken up into a number of smaller areas for special uses, but still presents an attractive appearance from the house. (This view, from above and to one side, would be seen only from a neighbour's attic window.) From the patio the view is bounded by the lefthand wall, the hedges and various trees and bushes, but the long vista across the lawn draws the eye and gives a sense of space. Hidden from the house are a work area, a play area and a vegetable plot.

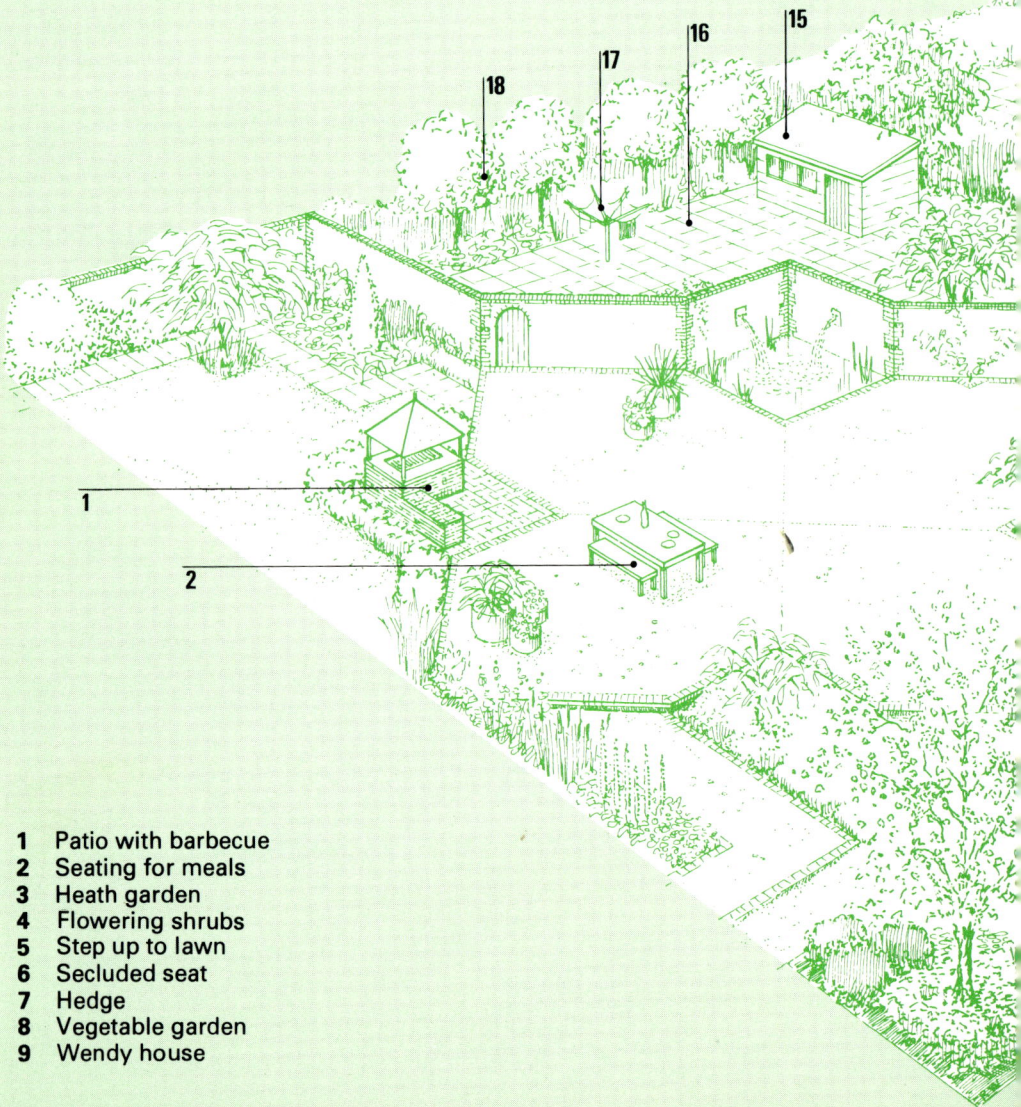

1 Patio with barbecue
2 Seating for meals
3 Heath garden
4 Flowering shrubs
5 Step up to lawn
6 Secluded seat
7 Hedge
8 Vegetable garden
9 Wendy house

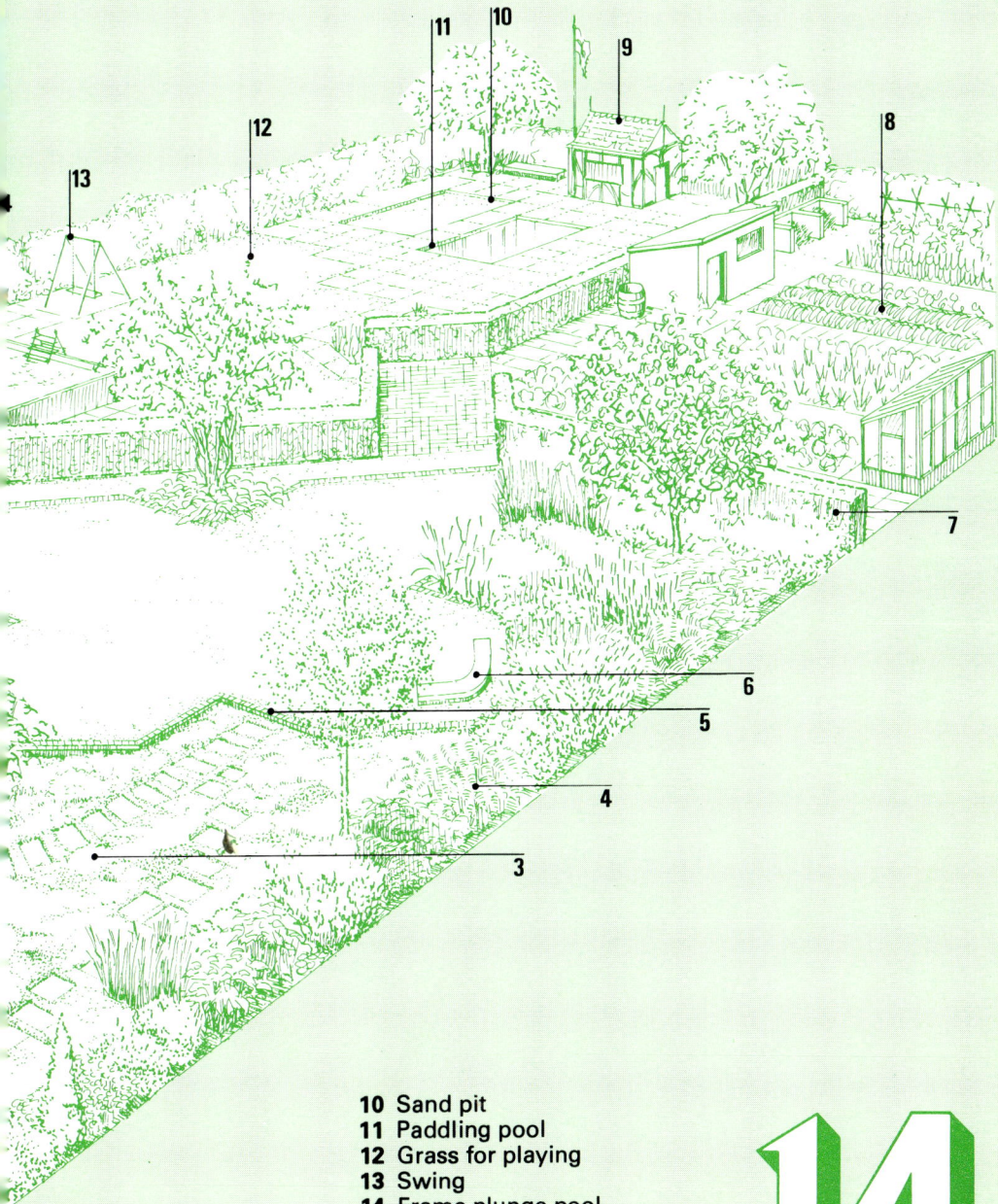

10 Sand pit
11 Paddling pool
12 Grass for playing
13 Swing
14 Frame plunge pool
15 Shed
16 Paved work area
17 Rotary clothes line
18 Fruit trees

14

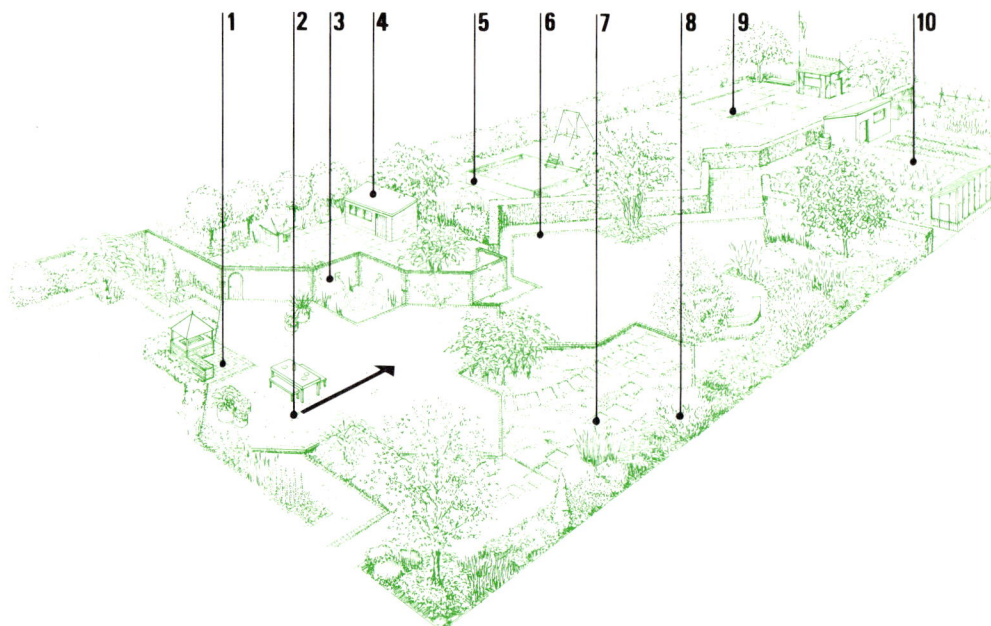

1
Barbecue stands on brick area, separating it from the patio of tinted exposed aggregate.

2
The main vista would be from the patio across the lawn, ending in the large trees and thick hedge.

3
Wall screens the work area, and backs the patio pool (pages 120–5), accommodating two small fountains.

4
Large shed could contain storage space for fruit from nearby trees.

5
Frame plunge pool, which is not built into the ground, will be easy to get rid of when children grow up (page 128).

6
Lawn edged with bricks or paved path for easier mowing.

7
Garden of heathers and heaths with stepping stones.

8
Flowering shrubs of varied heights, with a few trees.

9
Children's area, with small Wendy house, sandpit, swing, pools, and grassy and paved areas for games (page 117).

10
Vegetable garden with shed, greenhouse and compost heap.

There are many heaths and heathers, but most dislike lime.
Calluna vulgaris (Common moorland heather), many varieties, flowers August and September.
Erica carnea (Winter heath), red to white, October-February.

Erica cinerea (Bell heath), pink to dark purple, June-August.
Erica tetralix (Cross-leaved heath), pink to white, June-October.

Children in the garden

If children have part of the garden reserved for them, they are less likely to interfere with the vegetable patch or to trample the flower beds. Even a simple sandpit or a swing can give many hours of enjoyment to a child. Wendy houses can be bought or made, but even a tiny tent or a grassy corner among the bushes will provide a 'house' for an imaginative child. Young children will also get much pleasure from a paddling pool; here, the rest of the family have a separate larger pool too.

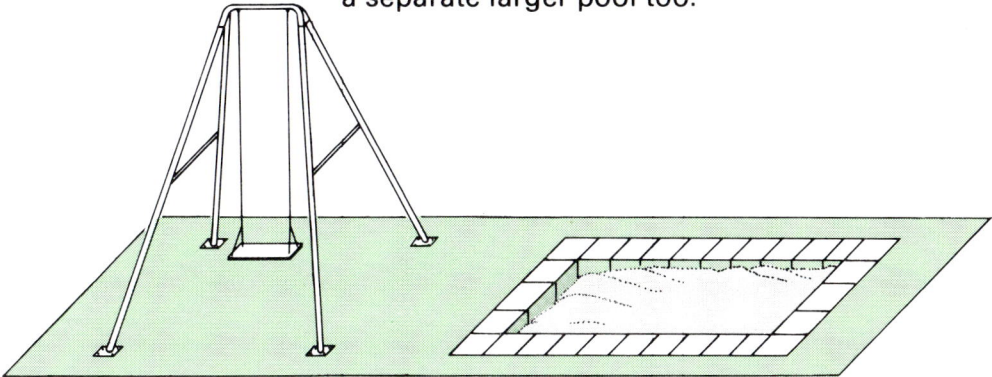

Most children enjoy having a swing, but you must make sure that it is safe. The frame must be fixed firmly into the ground, so that the whole thing does not topple over. If the seat is on ropes, these should be inspected regularly to see that they are not frayed or rotted.

A sandpit is better sunk in the ground, so that sand can be swept back into it from the area around it. Fill the bottom of a deep hole with rubble (for drainage), then cover with a deep layer of sea sand. The pit must have a lid of some sort, made of wood or wire netting, to keep cats out at night.

For appearances' sake it is pleasant to have a bed of flowers around the lawn, but if the lawn is meant for games, plant heather or creeping shrubs, which will not object to trampling feet as much as a bed of gladioli would! When the children get older, you can grow fragile blooms, and change the old sandpit into a new flowerbed.

If a lawn is intended for children to play on, you should choose very tough grass for the purpose, or it will be worn bare in no time (see pages 80–3). The lawn should be aerated often by spiking so that the hard-packed soil does not encourage the growth of mosses among the grass, which become slippery when wet.

Work areas

Many ordinary family activities have to be accommodated in the back garden. A washing line may be of the umbrella type or the long traditional sort, but the housewife needs to be able to reach it from a path or paved area. Rubbish bins and compost heaps help you to dispose tidily of house and garden refuse. Space must also be allowed for storing tools, including wheelbarrow and lawnmower, in a shed or large cupboard; and frames for seeds and cuttings will also be needed.

Most back gardens have some sort of clothes line, either the single long cord or the modern umbrella type. The long one may run along a straight path, but a circular one needs a large paved area; a lawn will be muddy in the winter. Avoid growing rose or holly bushes nearby, or the sheets may suffer.

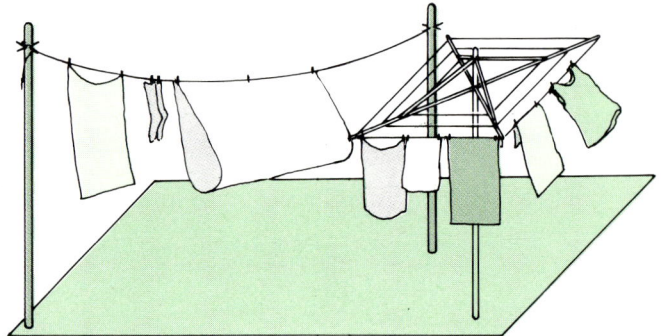

Ideally every gardener needs a shed for tools, a cold or warm frame or two, and a tap for watering, all within easy reach, and centred on a paved area where he can work even in bad weather. But many lovely gardens are made and maintained with less-than-perfect facilities, so do not despair.

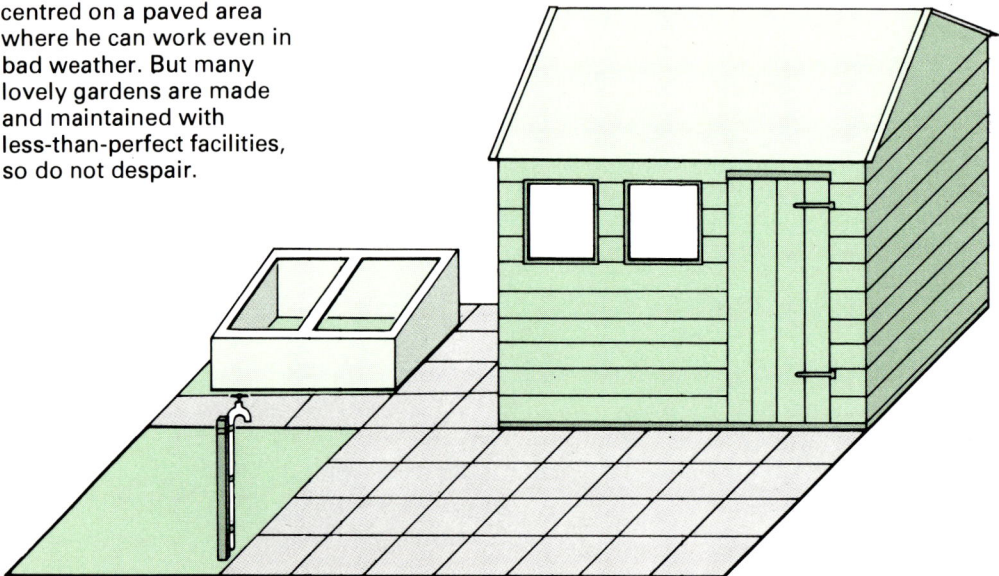

If space is limited in your garden, and you choose to have a wooden fence, why not build a tool cupboard onto the fence? Of course, it can be only a few inches deep, but this will be plenty for a garden hose, spades and forks, and small items, leaving the shed free for large items and for wet-weather jobs.

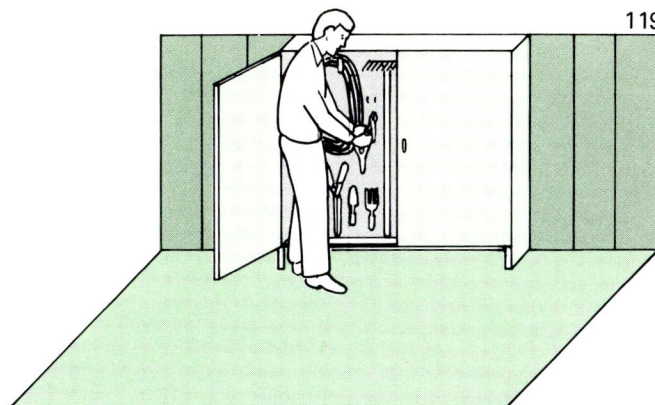

Many house owners feel that their garden looks better if they build some sort of enclosure around the dustbin. A hedge or fence may just screen the bin from the house, but a wooden container built for the purpose will also ensure that the bin is not tipped over by animals or by small children.

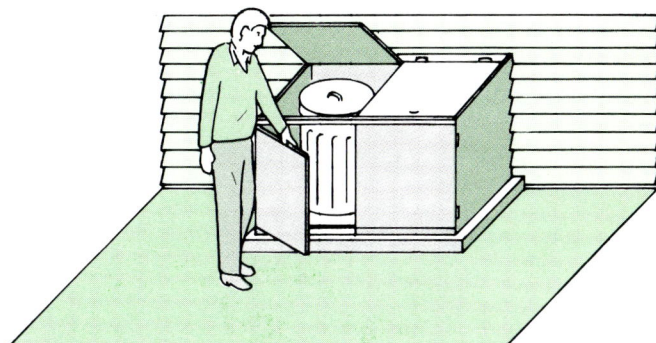

All gardens need a compost heap, and although it can be just a heap of refuse, a plastic bin makes a much neater corner. If you are a handyman, it is quite simple to build a small wooden bin to keep the heap within tidy limits.

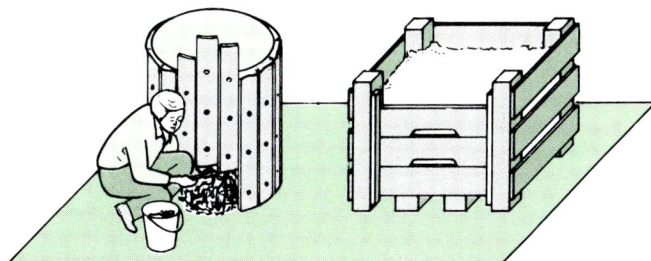

Compost can be made in your own garden, and if properly done, will be as useful as farmyard manure. Use any vegetable matter except diseased plants, flowered plants, hedge cuttings, brassica stalks, perennial weeds, or tough stems, or grass mowings recently treated with a herbicide. Don't use the remains of meat or fish.

Cross-section of compost heap

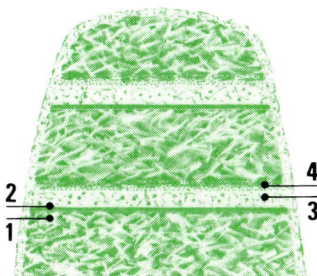

1 About 9 in (23 cm) of mixed vegetable refuse
2 A handful or two of sulphate of ammonia
3 About 2 in (5 cm) of soil
4 A sprinkling of lime
Repeat these layers until the heap is 4–5 ft (1.2–1.5 m) high, ending with vegetable refuse, and cover the whole heap with soil. Leave for 6–12 months before using.

A water garden

This is a garden for people who enjoy pools, streams and waterfalls. The constant movement of water on this gently sloping site is refreshing. In the series of four linked pools, a submerged pump in the fourth (and lowest) pool sucks in water through a filter, and then forces it up through an underground pipe to the waterfall above the first (top) pool, so that the same water travels round and round. Because the house is at the lowest point, the drainage must be expertly done, or the house will be damp.

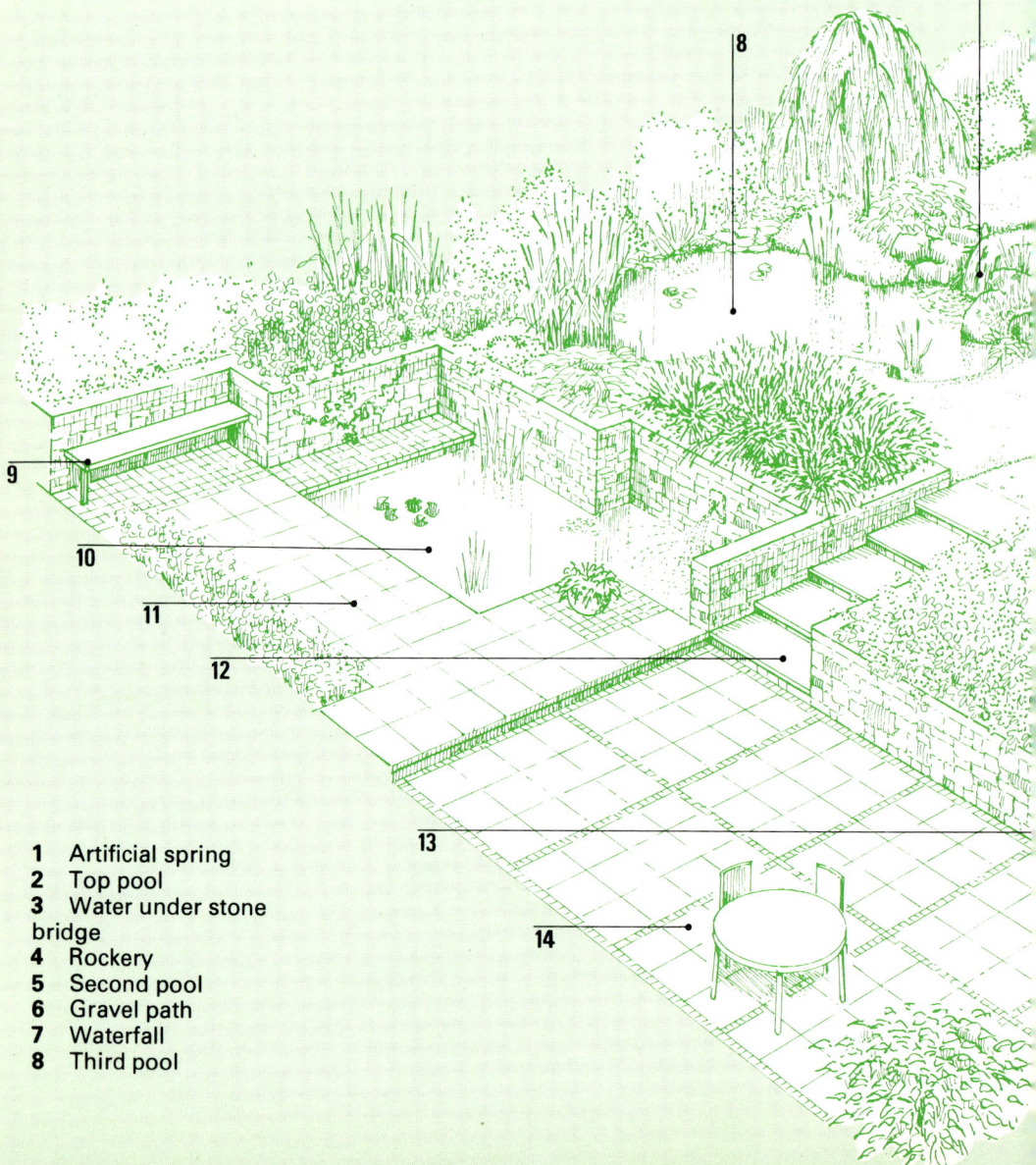

1 Artificial spring
2 Top pool
3 Water under stone bridge
4 Rockery
5 Second pool
6 Gravel path
7 Waterfall
8 Third pool

Weeds usually grow in open patches of garden. The more plants you have, the less weeds can find the space to grow in. Ground-cover plants are especially useful for keeping weeds out.

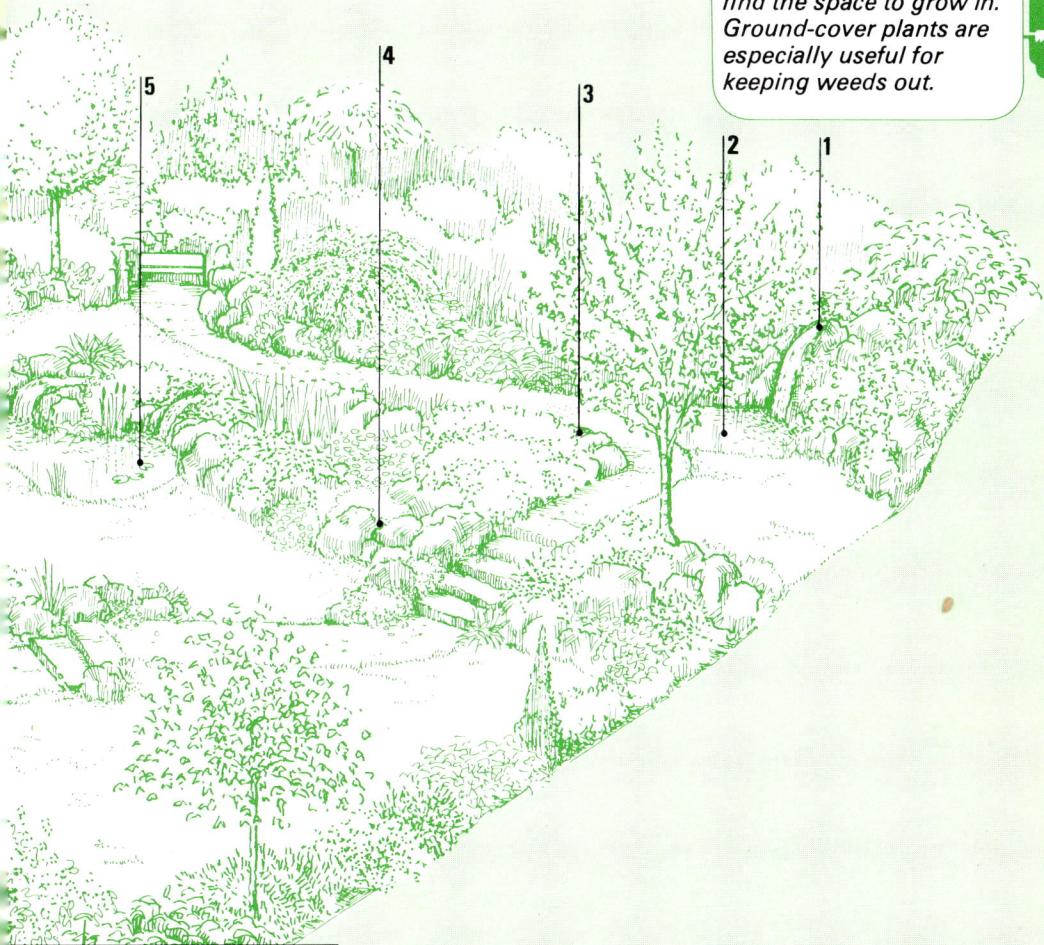

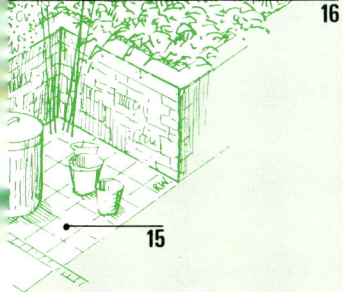

5
4
3
2
1
16
15

9 Seat
10 Fourth pool
11 Raised area
12 Broad steps
13 Natural stone wall
14 Patio
15 Dustbin area
16 Roses or other flowers

15

1
Raised area of patio gives interesting change of level and reduces amount of excavation needed for pool.
2
Water-loving plants growing around pool stop edges looking stiff and artificial (see below).
3
Fourth pool fed from third by fountain set in stone wall; pump submerged in pool near fountain must be removed in winter (say, October to April).
4
Third pool (lined with concrete or butyl rubber) fed from second pool by waterfall.

5
Small weeping tree such as Salix purpurea 'Pendula' planted not too near pool.
6
Natural stone wall made waterproof (with bitumen) on the rear side.
7
Grass or low ground cover such as Minuartia verna caespitosa.
8
Second pool, fed from top pool by stream under path, and low waterfall.
9
Secluded seat tucked away among built-up rockwork, forming pleasant suntrap.
10
First pool, fed from artificial spring by way of waterfall.

When you buy water plants you may be unable to plant them at once. They will keep for several days in the fridge, wrapped securely in polythene. But label them clearly, or they may get eaten by mistake!

1 Water lilies
These look exotic but are very hardy perennials. They like a lot of sun in summer, and dislike strong currents in the water, so place any pump near the water inlet. Water lilies are better planted in perforated containers (below right), then lowered into the pond; firm the soil down, and put a layer of pebbles over it.

The kind of water lily you choose for your pool must depend on the depth of the water in it. There are many varieties of Nymphaea, and their flowers may be from 2 in to 10 in (5–25 cm) across, in various shades of white, pink, red and yellow. Most of them flourish at a depth of between 10 in and 15 in (25–37 cm).

In a natural pond, water seeps out around the edges to create a marshy marginal area where bog plants grow. In an artificial pond, this does not happen, and if you want to grow marsh plants you must use a very broad shallow shelf inside the pool itself, building up the soil until it is above the surface of the water.

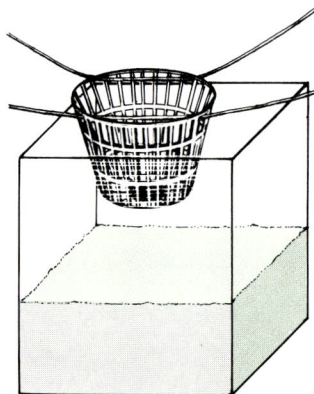

2 Marginal marsh plants
Calla palustris (Bog arum)
Eriophorum (Cotton grass)
Iris laevigata (Water iris)
Iris pseudacorus (Yellow flag)
Mimulus luteus (Monkey musk)
Ranunculus lingua grandiflora
Sagittaria sp. (Arrowheads)
Typha sp. (Reed mace, often wrongly called Bulrush)

3 Submerged water plants
If you intend to keep fish, a few of the following are necessary, to provide food, oxygen and shelter. Move them during the summer.
Callitriche (Water starwort)
Ceratophyllum (Hornwort)
Elodea canadensis
Myriophyllum spicatum (Water milfoil)
Ranunculus aquatilis (Water crowfoot)

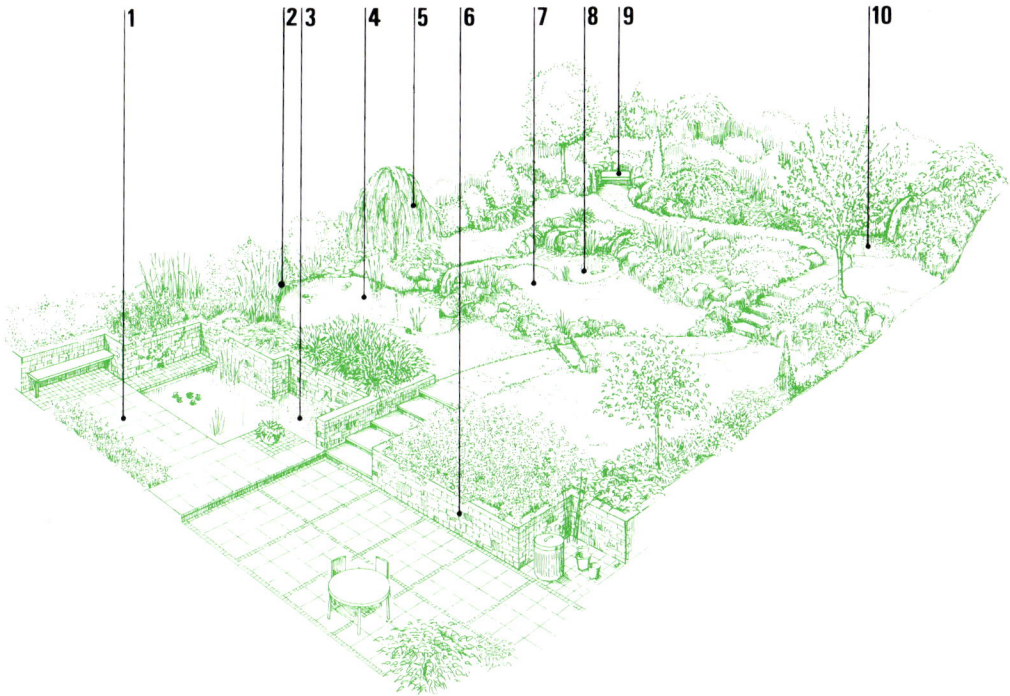

4 Insects
Your pond will soon fill up with insect life. Many insects fly in, including beetles, midges, dragonflies and moths. Other insects arrive among the plants you buy. Most of these will be harmless, many beneficial. Some species will prey on other insects and keep them down; and most will serve as food for your fish.

Many insects lay eggs in or on the water, and larvae later hatch from these. Both eggs and larvae are food for many kinds of fish, as are the adult insects too. On the other hand, some large water insects eat the eggs of fish. And both insects and fish may also eat the leaves of submerged water plants.

5 Fish
Once the water plants are thriving, you can buy goldfish, shubunkins, golden orfe or other hardy pond fish. In an established pond with plenty of plants and insects there is no need to feed fish artificially. A few water snails will help to keep the pool clean by eating decaying vegetation.

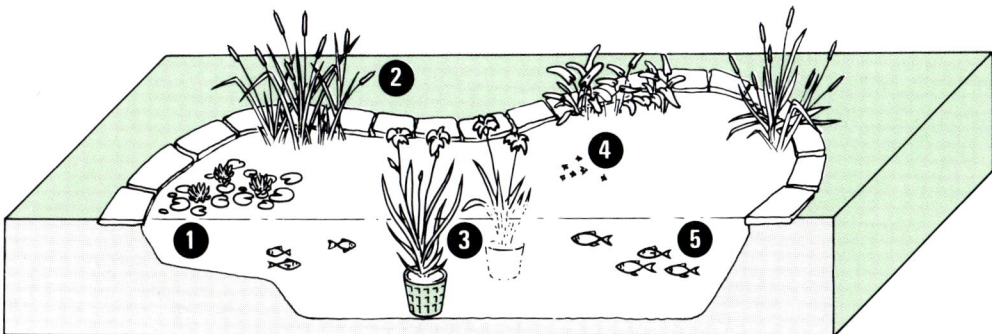

Ponds

Garden ponds and pools are easy to construct, allowing water plants to grow and providing the ideal setting for fountains, waterfalls and cascades. There are several ways to construct a pond. Plastic sheeting is the most convenient and adaptable, and after a few days looks entirely natural. Concrete basins tend to crack and leak in cold weather. Preformed fibreglass units are easy to install but expensive, and do not allow much flexibility in shape and size.

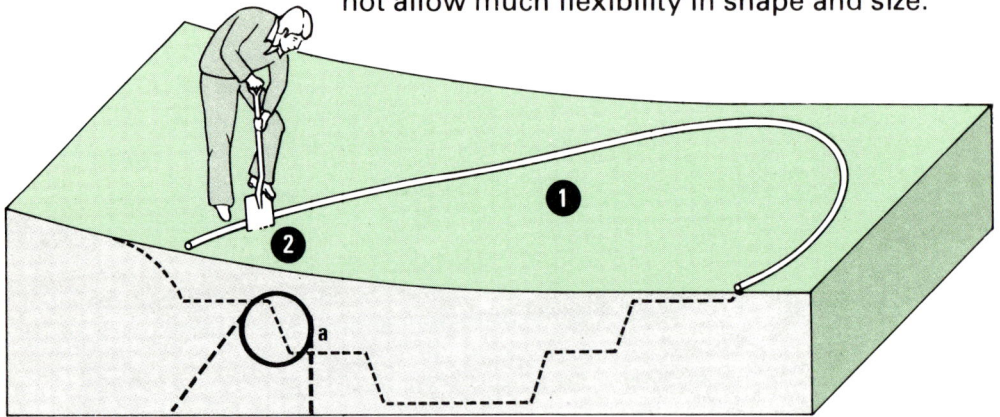

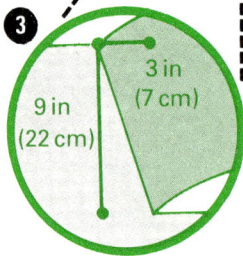

3 in
(7 cm)

9 in
(22 cm)

Building a pool with plastic liner
1 Mark out the shape and size of the pool with hosepipe or rope.
2 Cut around the outline with a spade.
3 Dig the pool with an inward slope of 3 in (7 cm) for every 9 in (22 cm) down. Make a marginal shelf for plants.

4 Check the level of the pool with a spirit level. Check the width and depth.
5 Remove sharp objects. Cover with a layer of moist sand to produce a smooth surface all over.

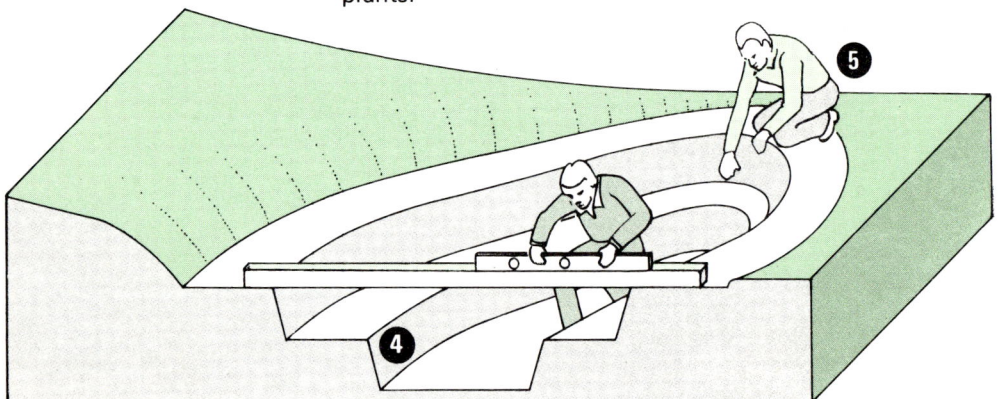

When choosing a site for your pond, avoid trees and shrubs, or falling leaves will be a nuisance. Depending on surface area, ponds should be dug to a depth of 15–30 in (37–75 cm). When the pond is filled, water plants and then fish can be added. Water plants maintain a balance in the pool and keep algae in check. They are better planted in submersible plastic containers than straight into soil laid on the shelves and the base of the pool.

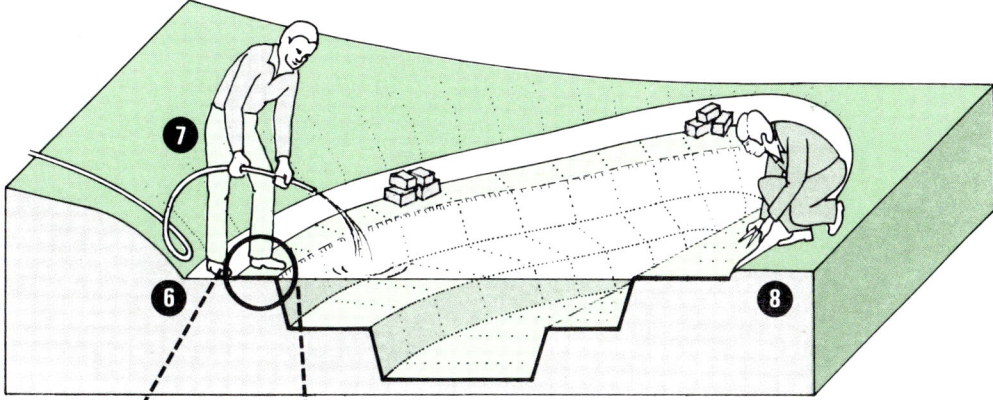

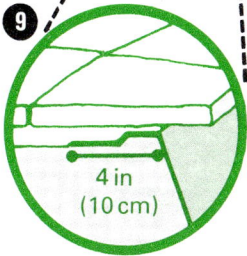

4 in
(10 cm)

6 Place the liner into the hole and weight the corners.
7 Fill the pool, easing corner weights to allow the liner to fit closely.
8 Trim liner to 4 in (10 cm) from edge. Secure if necessary.

9 Lay a paving surround on a mortar base, leaving an overhang of 2 in (5cm). Alternatively, make a turfed edge by fitting the liner into an angled slit cut 6 in (15 cm) from the rim and placing turf on top, allowing overhang.
10 Install fountains, build rockeries, add water plants and fish.

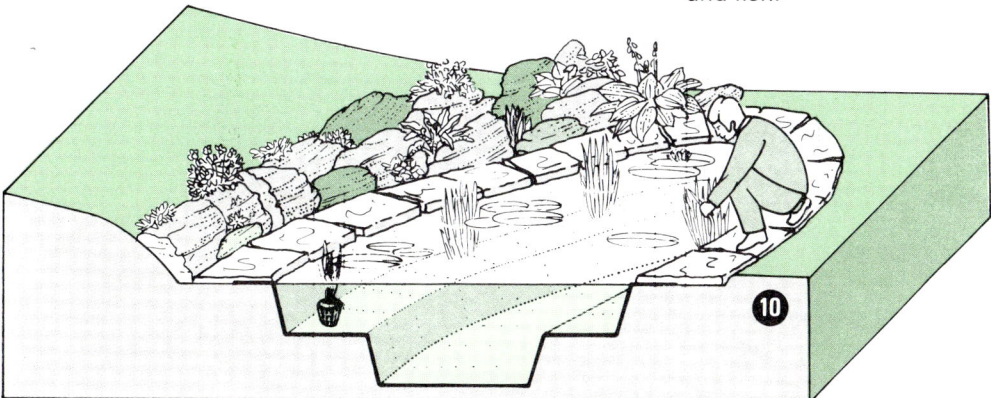

A swimming-pool garden

This design could be either an entire garden or part of a very much larger one. The garden is centred on an oval-shaped swimming pool, with an oval non-slip path around it. Beyond the pool a complex of buildings provides outdoor but roofed sitting space, an enclosed sitting area with glass doors (useful for windy days), a pump room and filtration building, and a changing room/sauna. Close beside the adult swimming pool is a children's shallow pool. Much of the rest of the garden consists of lawns.

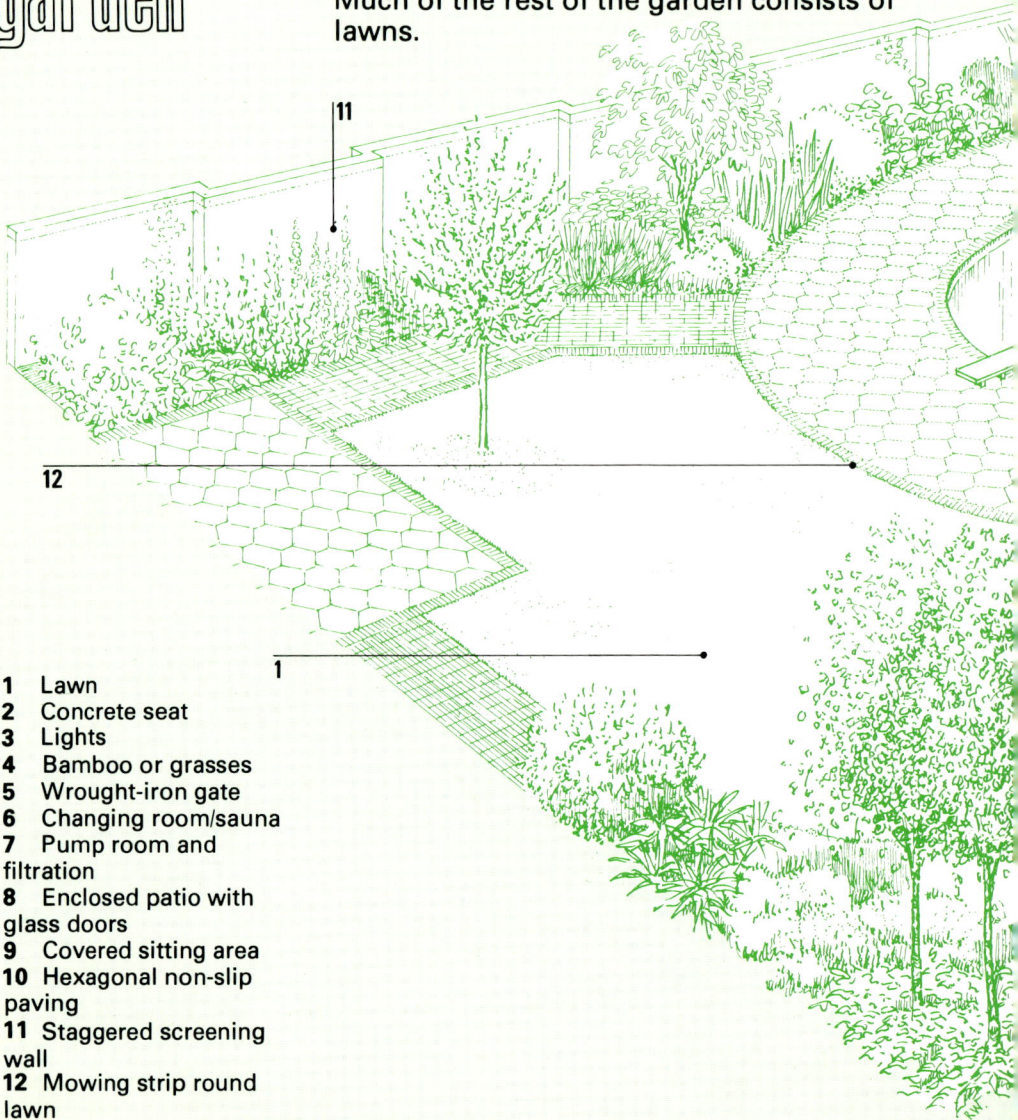

1 Lawn
2 Concrete seat
3 Lights
4 Bamboo or grasses
5 Wrought-iron gate
6 Changing room/sauna
7 Pump room and filtration
8 Enclosed patio with glass doors
9 Covered sitting area
10 Hexagonal non-slip paving
11 Staggered screening wall
12 Mowing strip round lawn

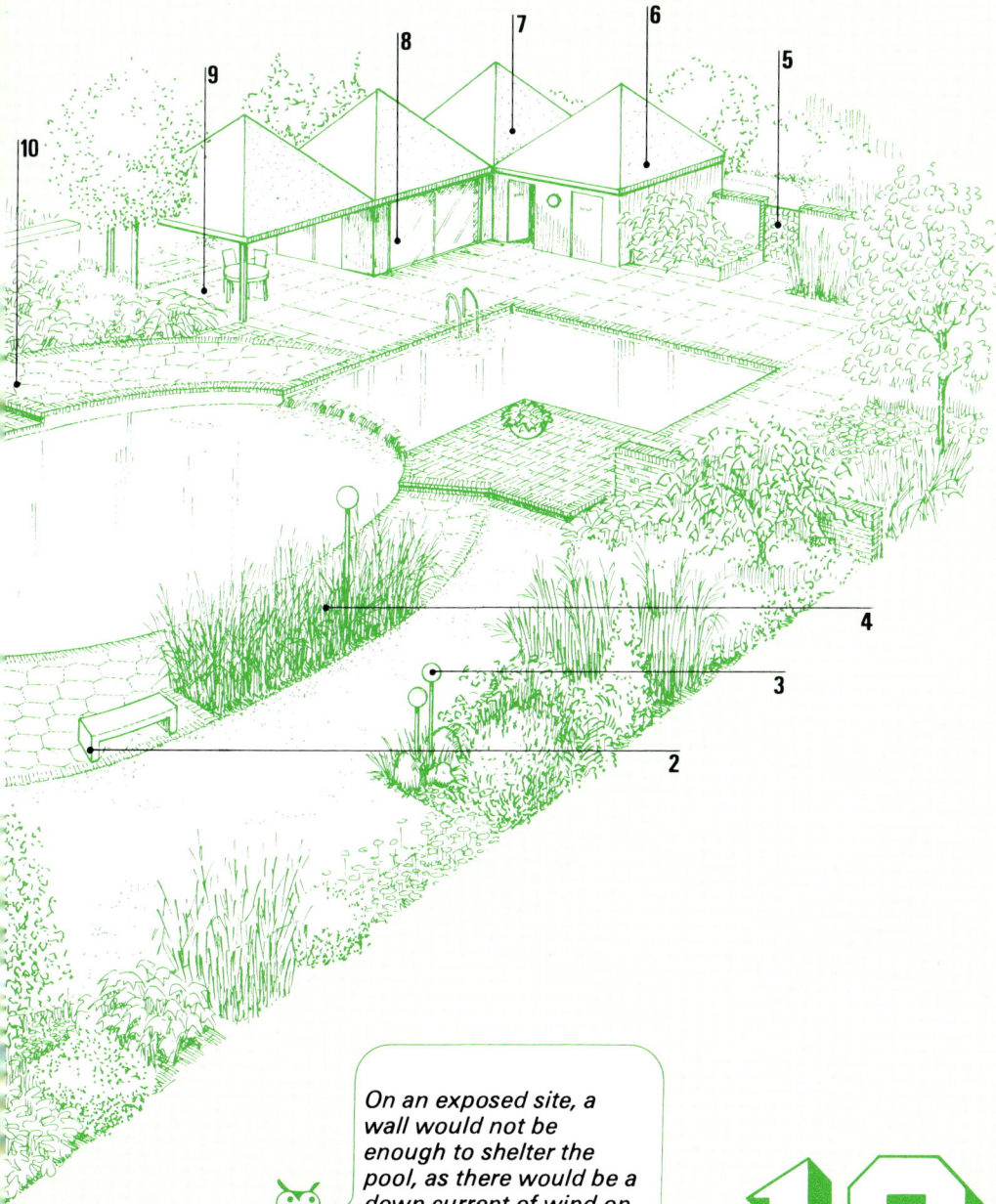

On an exposed site, a wall would not be enough to shelter the pool, as there would be a down current of wind on the near side. It would need a screen of trees or shrubs on the far side of the wall too.

16

Swimming pools

Most people enjoy lazing in or near a swimming pool in hot sunny weather. But before you rush to build one, consider carefully what you want it for. If it is for a toddler, a small inflatable plastic pool is plenty, and easy to get rid of later. But if you have a potential Olympic swimmer in the family, and unlimited funds, a large concrete structure may be more suitable. Remember that most large pools take a lot of upkeep, and that you will be able to use them for only a few months each year. They will need some sort of

Most pools take up a lot of garden space, and are used for only a short time each summer. A small pool makes less demands on space and cash, and is far easier to remove when not wanted.

1 The most usual pool for a family with young children is a small, simple inflatable plastic one, which can be bought quite cheaply. It can be emptied, dried, deflated and stored away until the next fine day. This is fine for toddlers to splash about in, but no use for adults.

2 The next size of pool is usually circular, made of steel and aluminium, and lined with vinyl. It can be 4 ft deep, and up to 24 ft across. The steps can be taken away to prevent accidents if you have small children. Such pools are used above ground, so you will not need to move masses of earth.

3 You can build a larger rectangular pool from prefabricated rigid sections, made of timber and steel, and lined with vinyl; the vinyl lining lasts for several years. Such pools can be sunk below ground level, but this enables leaves to blow in easier! Non-slip paving is then necessary around the pool edges.

4 If you have plenty of money, you can build a large concrete pool, but this must be drained in winter, or ice may crack the concrete. Regular treatment is needed to kill algae, which cause a slippery green slime to grow; a filter unit and occasional chlorination are needed for large pools.

filter unit to keep the water clean, and it is very wise also to have a water heater: although these are fairly expensive to run, they ensure that you can get much more use out of the pool than if you have to wait for the water to warm up naturally. Even now the expense is not over, however, for there are also accessories such as steps into the pool, some sort of skimming device to remove insects and debris from the pool surface, and a cover for the pool to keep the warmth in the water.

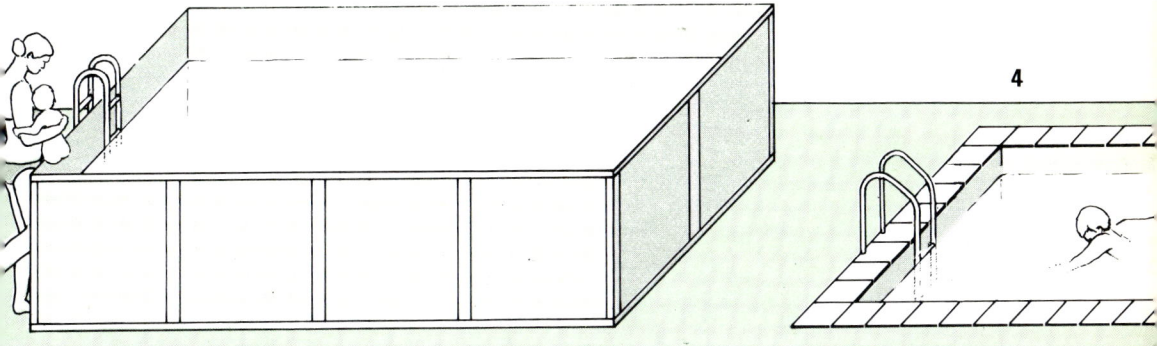

4

a Remember that your swimming pool must fit into the rest of the garden. Have some sort of path between a lawn and the pool, for easy mowing and safety. Site the pool where the prevailing winds will *not* blow leaves and debris into the water. And try to have some other focus of attention for when the pool will be out of use.

b Try to site your swimming pool in a sunny corner, so that the sun will warm the water and the swimmers. If you can use it only in the late afternoon or evening in the week, this is especially important, because it can get chilly towards evening. A hedge on the windy side will also help to make your bathe more comfortable.

c If you want to get plenty of use out of your pool, you will need to arrange for some sort of heating. The cost of installing and running depends on the size of the pool and the sort of fuel you choose: electricity is the most expensive way of heating the water, but the machinery costs less.

d If you make a new pool, you will probably also acquire a lot of visitors (with swimsuits). Unless you want wet footprints across the dining-room carpet, you should think out carefully where they (and you) can change clothes after a swim; this may involve building a special changing room, or adapting your home.

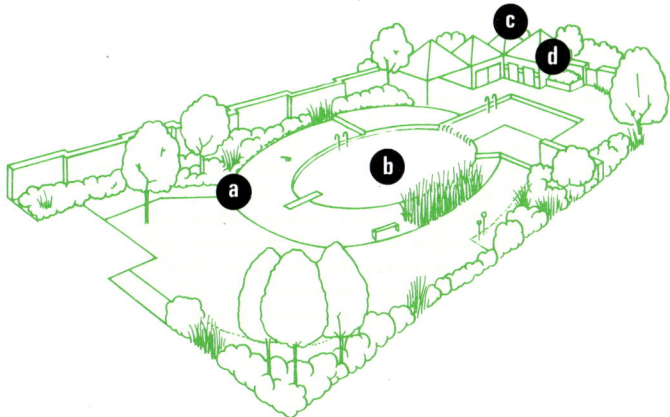

A problem garden

This pleasant garden has been built around two awkward fixtures: an electricity sub-station and a large patch of concrete. First a high fence was built to help disguise the sub-station, and trees and shrubs were planted near it. Then an attractive rustic screen was built, giving tempting glimpses of the rest of the garden through it, and directing the eye to one of two main vistas, through the two arches of the trellis. Finally, the concrete was surrounded with plants, many of them horizontal.

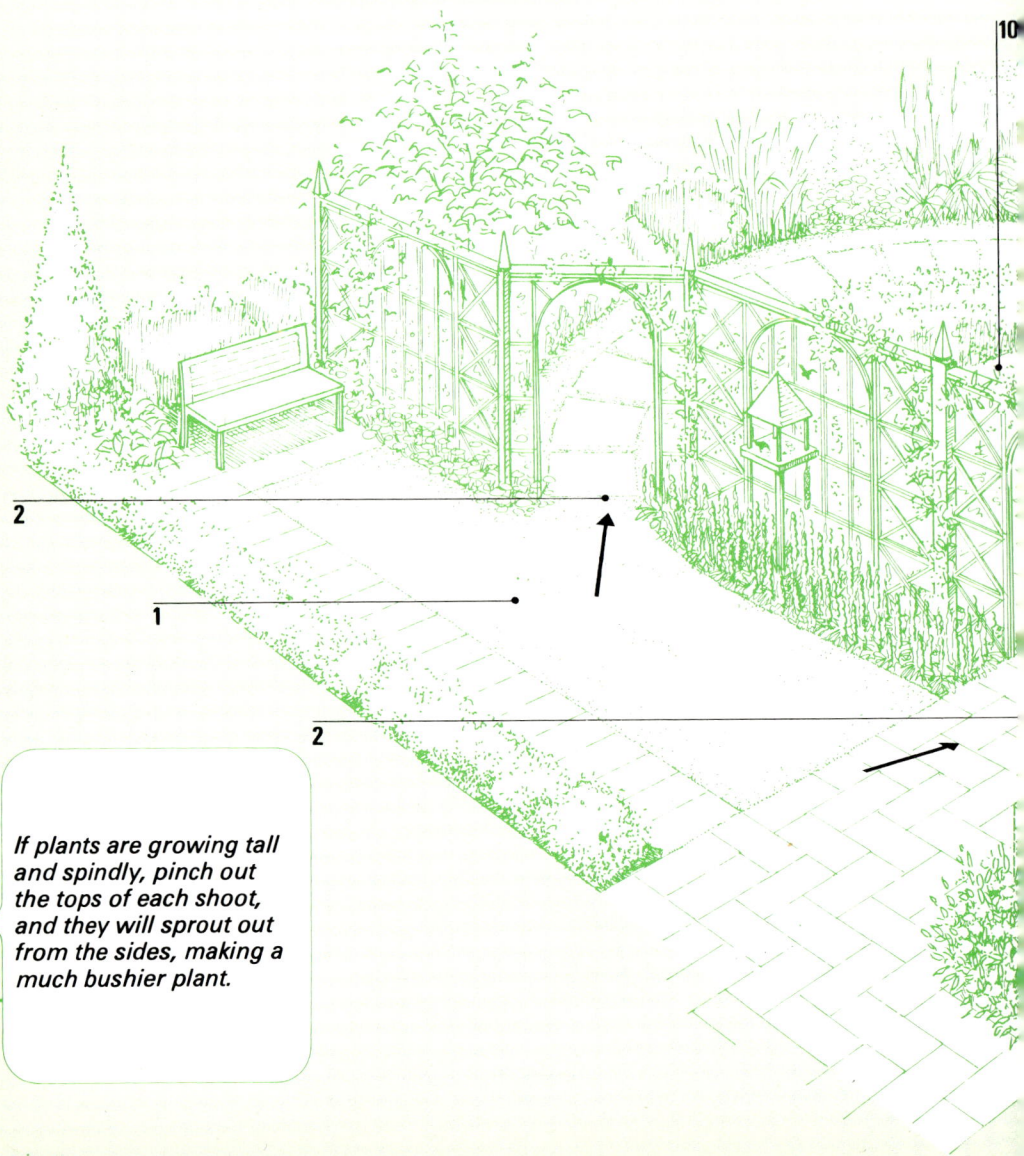

If plants are growing tall and spindly, pinch out the tops of each shoot, and they will sprout out from the sides, making a much bushier plant.

1 Lawn
2 Two vistas from house
3 Dustbin container
4 Focal point
5 Columnar conifer
6 Small weeping tree
7 Small utility area
8 Electricity sub-station
9 Tree
10 Concrete area

17

1
Trellis not too near the house, to avoid darkening rooms.

2
The trellis should not be too closely covered, except at the bottom (to hide the concrete). Use climbing (*not* rambling) roses, Clematis alpina, Solanum crispum, or Hedera helix 'Glacier'.

3
Note the clever angling of the trellis, so that the eye is directed around the mass of concrete; if the trellis had been straight across the garden, the left-hand arch would have pointed almost directly at the eyesore.

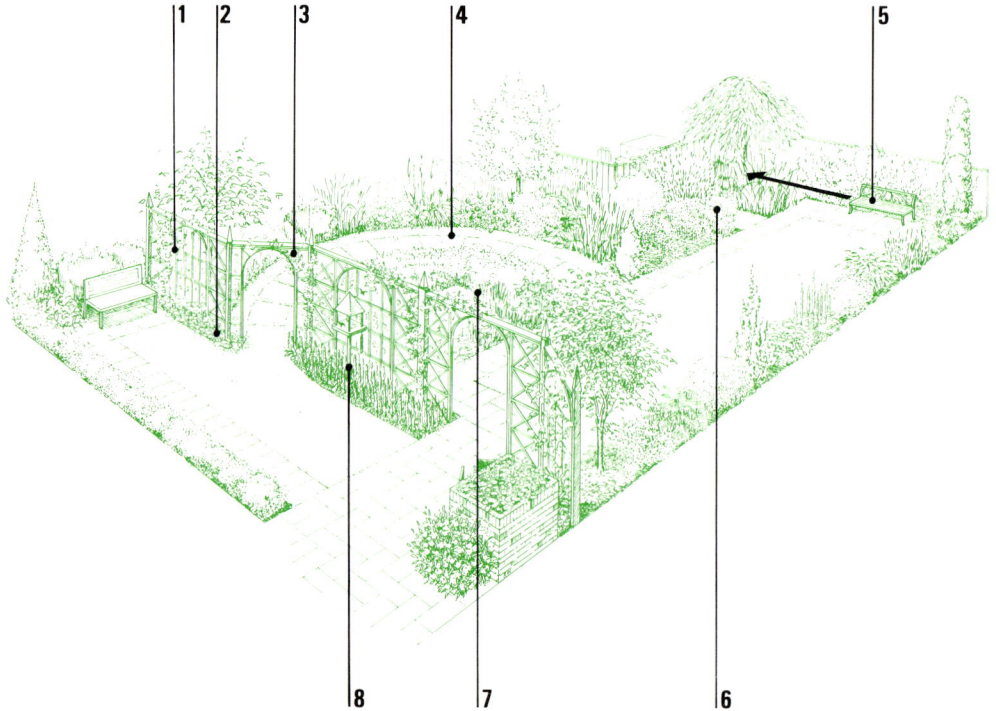

4
Curved path looks mysterious from house, and directs the eye around the concrete mass.

5
View from seat does not include sub-station (hidden by tree), and seat provides focal point for whole garden.

6
Small paved utility area hidden away behind tall shrubs.

7
Concrete area may be air raid shelter, shed foundation, cess pit cover or inspection cover; disguise depends on whether it is still in use.

8
Bird table near the house, so that birds can be easily fed in winter weather (when they most need it).

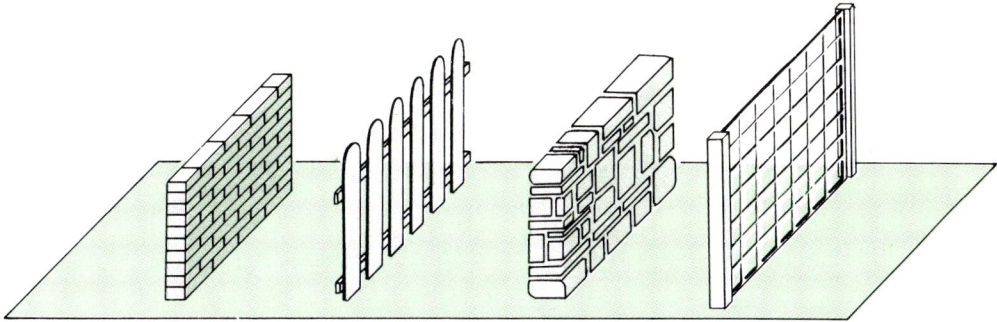

If you have an eyesore in your garden, there are three possible ways to cope with it. If you *can* get rid of it, that is the best solution. But if it is a fixture, you can either hide it behind another object (eg fence, tree) or distract attention from it to another focus. In many cases it is best to use both these methods.

Fences and walls (above) hide any low object completely, but this may mean that they make the house or part of the garden dark. It may also be an expensive solution in some circumstances. Lattice fences or a trellis, with a climbing plant or two, will often do the job as well, but may leave your ugly secret revealed in winter.

Bushes or trees may also be used to disguise an unsightly feature in or near your garden. But again you may find that in winter the leaves will fall and the eyesore is back with you again. Evergreens are one answer. But you may find that you do not spend enough time outdoors in winter for it to matter.

Many an ugly feature has been turned into an asset by a little imagination. A large tree stump covered with roses or clematis is a splendid centrepiece. An old pigsty can be converted to a playhouse for a child. And many a rockery started life as a pile of rubble. Visitors will see only the finished thing, not its ugly beginning.

If the ugly feature that worries you is a large block of flats, there will probably be little you can do to hide it away. The most you can hope for is to plan secluded corners of the garden where you can sit without being seen from the flats and where your pleasant view does not include them (see pages 60–1).

A garden for retirement

This is a garden designed for those who are unable (or unwilling) to do much energetic gardening. The broad curved paths would be convenient for anyone in a wheelchair, and the raised beds could be tended from a wheelchair or by someone unable to bend much. The lawn

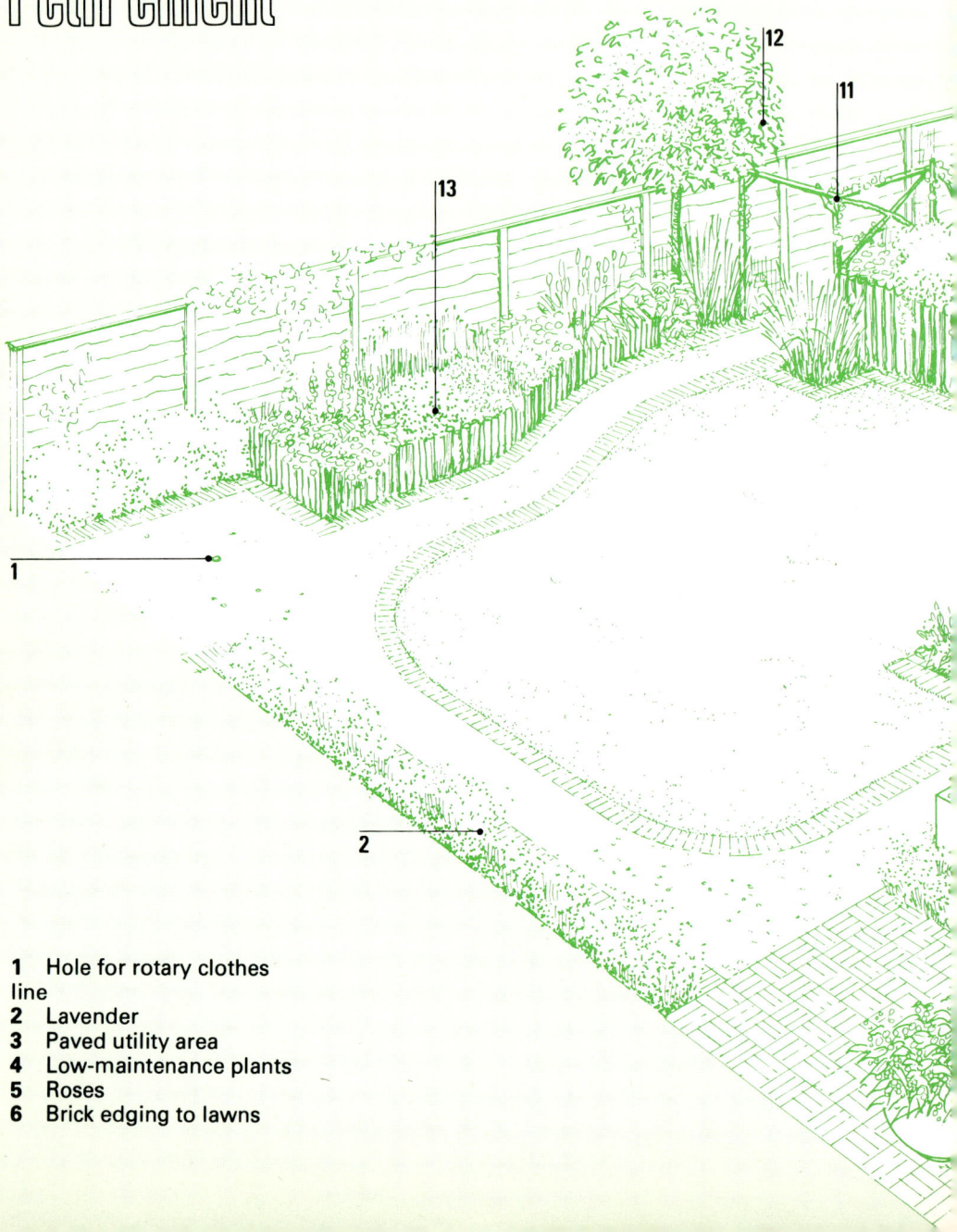

1   Hole for rotary clothes line
2   Lavender
3   Paved utility area
4   Low-maintenance plants
5   Roses
6   Brick edging to lawns

is possible for an elderly person to cut, with the help of modern machines, and the broad edging makes the maintenance of its shape easy. A small secluded vegetable patch makes it possible for the gardener to produce some homegrown foods.

7 Concrete or tarmac path
8 Seat as focal point
9 Vegetable patch
10 Fan-trained fruit trees
11 Rustic trellis
12 Tree gives height
13 Raised borders

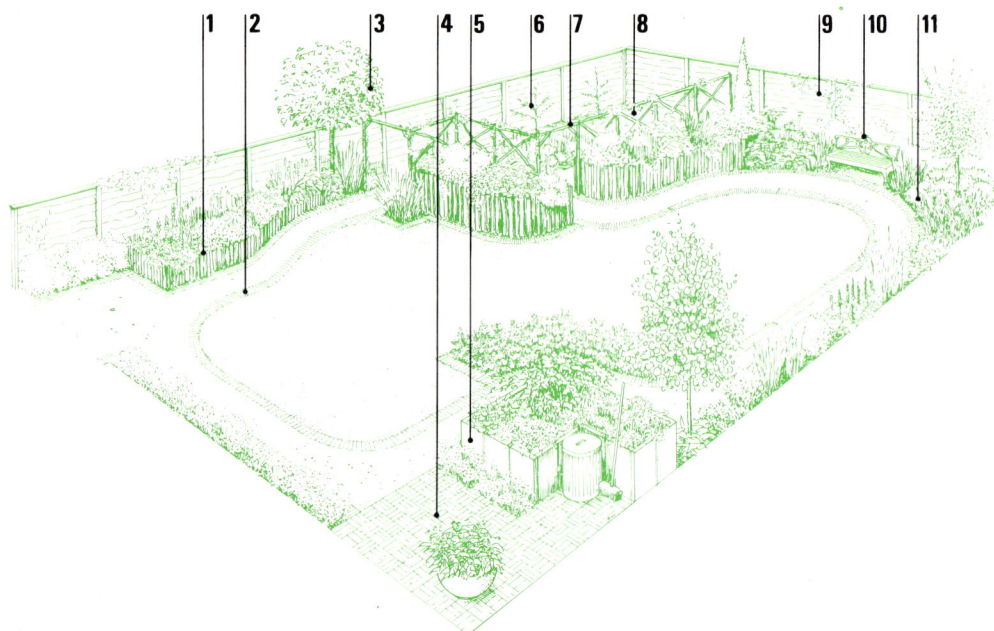

1
Raised beds, inexpensively made with logs, can be tended from a wheelchair.
2
Brick edging should be ½ in (1 cm) below level of lawn for easy mowing.
3
Tree varies height, and breaks up the long expanse of fence.
4
Paved utility area, with dustbin hidden from garden but handy for kitchen door.

5
Inexpensive wall of paving slabs set into concrete to make a raised bed.
6
Fan-trained fruit trees are easy to reach for pruning and harvesting.
7
Rustic trellis for vines, climbing plants or even runner beans.

8
Small vegetable patch is enough for an elderly person to grow salads or a few vegetables.
9
Climbers on fence.
10
Seat as focal point, and a useful stopping place on a tour of the garden.
11
Permanent low-maintenance planting, mostly shrubs (see opposite) or trouble-free herbaceous plants.

When gardening, don't do a whole morning's digging, or several hours' repotting. Break up your day into an hour of one kind of work, then an hour of another kind. This is easier on the muscles, and more interesting.

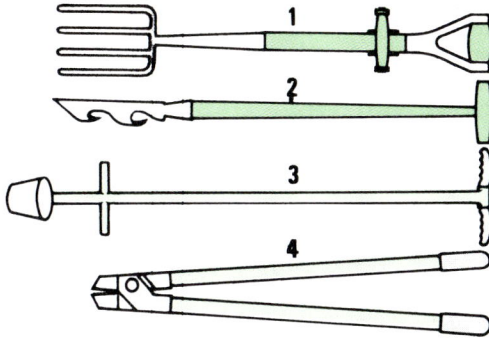

There are many useful tools (not all of them specially designed for handicapped gardeners) that can make chores easier, including:
1 fork with extra handle grip to give leverage;
2 weed extractor for really long-rooted weeds;
3 bulb planter;
4 long-handled secateurs.

There are many lightweight spades and forks available, some with special handle grips for the disabled gardener. Wheelbarrows have been made that can be towed along from a wheelchair. There are also several kinds of kneelers and stools for elderly people who are able to use them but need a handle to help them down and up.

There are a number of long-handled secateurs available, intended for pruning trees and shrubs, and these are even more useful to the wheelchair gardener than to the able-bodied one. Such tools vary in length, but may reach 29 in (73 cm), and weight around 3 lb (1.3 kg). But many shrubs need only occasional attention.

For wheelchair users, paths must be fairly broad, with a good firm surface (*not* gravel). Gentle curves are better than sharp corners, and arches must be plenty wide enough. Steps must of course be avoided, but a gentle slope is negotiable. Unsteady elderly people need a firm path that does not get slippery when wet.

Apart from selecting tools to help him with the job, the handicapped gardener can also choose his plants to fit his needs. A blind person can enjoy scented flowers, but coloured ones give him little pleasure. And by selecting shrubs that need little tending, a wheelchair gardener can lighten his pruning chores.

Scented flowers that a blind person can enjoy
Honeysuckle
Jasmine
Lavender
Lilac
Mignonette
Roses
Stock
Sweet peas
Thyme
Wallflowers

Shrubs that need little pruning
Acer
Berberis
Camellia
Cotoneaster
Daphne
Euonymus
Genista
Magnolia
Mahonia
Pyracantha

Vegetable gardens

If you are aiming to have a beautiful garden, you may choose to site the vegetables at the far end from the house, behind a hedge or barrier of some sort. On the other hand, many cooks like to have the vegetable patch near their kitchen door, to avoid a long damp trek on a rainy day to gather just one lettuce or a single cabbage. But it is usually possible to grow at least a few common herbs near the kitchen door, because they are acceptable in any flower garden.

The vegetable garden should face south, or be sheltered on the north side, and must be well-drained. If one piece of land is used every year, plan a rotation so that the same crop is not grown in the same place: plant potatoes, swedes or leeks in Year 1; peas, beans, carrots or beetroot in Year 2; and brassicas (cabbage, sprouts, cauliflower) in Year 3.

If you follow this 3-year rotation, the plot must be prepared beforehand: Year 1, manure heavily; Year 2, feed little; Year 3, manure in autumn, then lime in winter. This does not mean that you must grow *only* potatoes in Year 1: you can have three separate plots, one at Year 1 of the rotation, one at Year 2, and one at Year 3.

Even quite a small patch of garden can produce enough vegetables to vary the family's diet and save a bit of money. If you grow only a small crop, you should harvest early, before the main crop arrives in the greengrocer's shop, to enjoy (say) new potatoes at their best, while they are expensive to buy; you can then buy, if you must, when they become cheap and plentiful. And many gardeners enjoy the luxury of asparagus at a fraction of what it would cost at the shop.

Keep a careful record of what you grow in each part of the garden, and what treatment you give the soil. If you plant potatoes in a bed that was limed the year before, you may get a crop of scabbed potatoes. And carrots will develop split roots in recently manured soil. With a record, you can give each variety the soil conditions it needs.

Do not plant your whole crop at once, or they will all be ready to harvest at the same time. Plant a few, then wait a week or 10 days and plant some more: this ensures a supply of young vegetables over several weeks. Grow a number of varieties, which may mature at different times, and will give your family a change of flavour.

Such fast-growing crops as radishes, lettuce and spring onions may be planted between the rows of your main crops, such as potatoes or peas, and will be ready for gathering before the main crop has grown large enough to need the space they occupy. Plant both cos lettuce and cabbage lettuce, and red and white radishes, for variety.

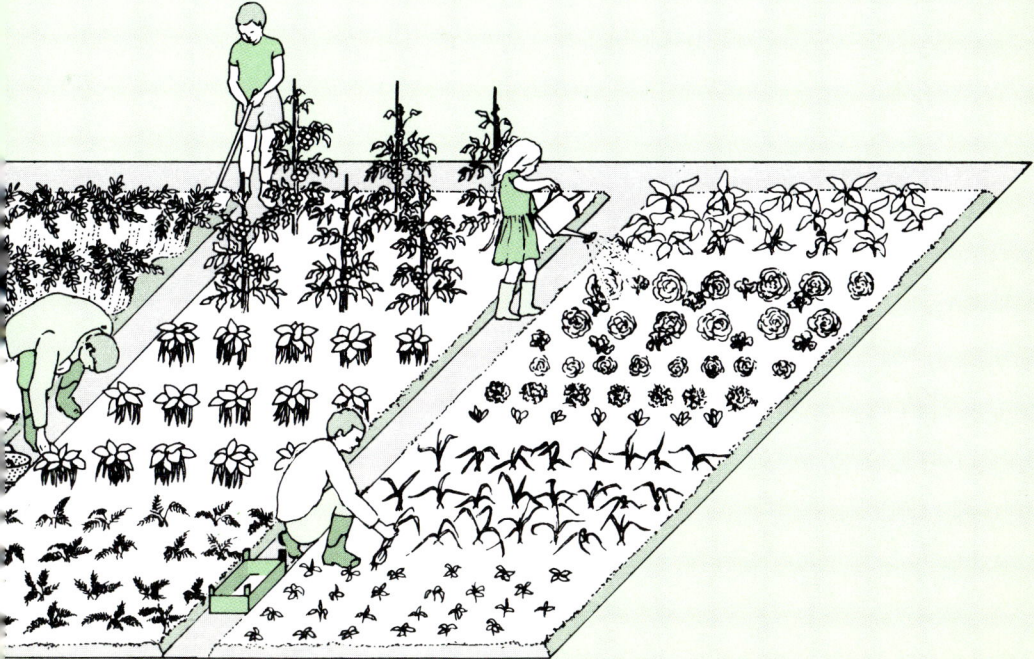

Facts and figures

Don't flinch at the sight of metric tables. Lots of splendid gardeners don't understand them either! But they may help you to lay out the design of the garden, to order fertilizer or concrete in the correct amounts, and to cope with the minor problems that sometimes arise. There is no exam at the end – but if you buy too little concrete to make that new path, it could be rather awkward, especially on Sunday morning, when you can't rush out to buy more. The best plan is to check any calculations twice, or to get your child to help.

With the U.K. half way to going metric, it is often necessary to convert amounts, which is usually a matter of simple multiplication. If you have already made a lot of concrete, though, you will probably know by experience how much water to add, etc. If you must do sums, make sure to keep the result, to save doing the same sums next year.

Unit	U.K. to metric	Metric to U.K.
Length	1 in = 2.5 cm 1 ft = 30 cm 1 yd = 0.9 m	1 cm = 0.4 in 1 m = 39 in
Area	1 sq in = 6.4 sq cm 1 sq ft = 0.1 sq m 1 sq yd = 0.8 sq m 1 acre = 0.4 hectare	1 sq cm = 0.2 sq in 1 sq m = 10.8 sq ft 1 hectare = 2.47 acres
Weight	1 oz = 28 g 1 lb = 0.45 kg 1 st = 6.3 kg 1 cwt = 50.8 kg	100 g = 3.5 oz 1 kg = 2.2 lb
Volume	1 cu in = 16.4 cc 1 cu ft = 0.03 cu m 1 cu yd = 0.8 cu m	1 cc = 0.061 cu in 1 cu m = 35.5 cu ft 1 cu m = 1 stere = 1.3 cu yd
Liquids	1 pt = 0.6 litre 1 qt = 1.1 litres 1 gall = 4.5 litres	1 litre = 1.8 pt

To mark out straight rows for planting seeds, use two wooden sticks and a length of string, then use the back of a rake to make a drill (shallow trench). To mark out a circular area (such as the lawn on page 37) you can also use the same apparatus, making sure you keep the string straight as you move it around the centre stick.

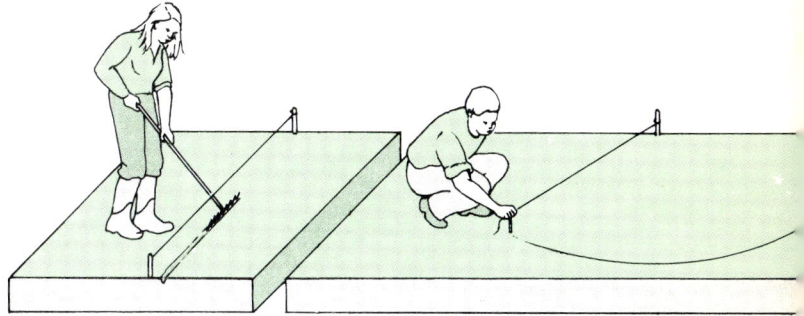

To calculate an irregular area, first measure it very carefully, then draw it on a piece of paper to a handy scale, say 1 in to 1 ft. Then divide up the drawn shape as nearly as possible into oblong pieces, find the area of each, and add them all together. It will obviously help all your calculations if you choose an easy shape!

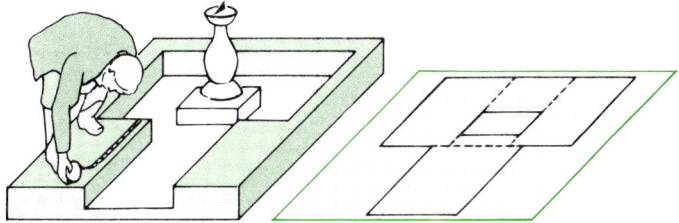

Distances apart (after thinning) of various vegetables:

	between plants	between rows
broad beans	9 in	1½ ft
dwarf French beans kidney	6 in	1½ ft
runner beans	9 in	15 in
beetroot	8 in	15 in
broccoli	2 ft	2 ft
brussels sprouts	2 ft	3 ft
spring cabbage	1–1½ ft	2 ft
winter cabbage	2 ft	2 ft
carrots	6 in	15 in
cauliflower	2 ft	2 ft
leeks	9 in	1½ ft
lettuce	10 in	15 in
onions	6 in	1 ft
parsnips	9 in	1½ ft
peas	4 in	depends on variety
potatoes	1 ft	2–2½ ft
radishes	3 in	6 in
spinach	1 ft	1 ft
swedes	1½ ft	1½ ft
tomatoes	1½ ft	2½ ft
turnips	9 in	1½ ft

Vegetables need varying amounts of space. Radishes can be put close together, whereas cabbages need room to spread. This table gives a rough idea how far apart your plants should be. But gardeners often plant many seeds and pull out the weak ones as they grow, leaving only the strongest ones to complete their development.

planning your garden

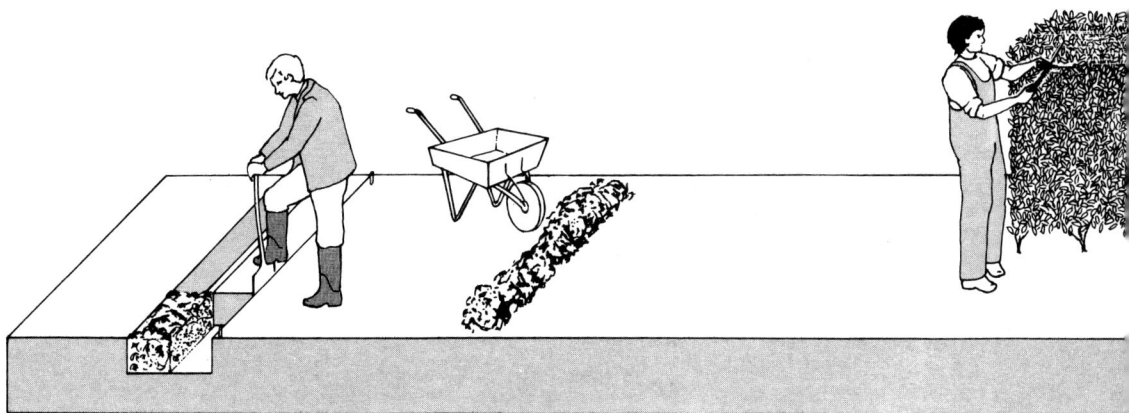

planni
your g